CONTEMPORARY ARAB POLITICS

A Concise History

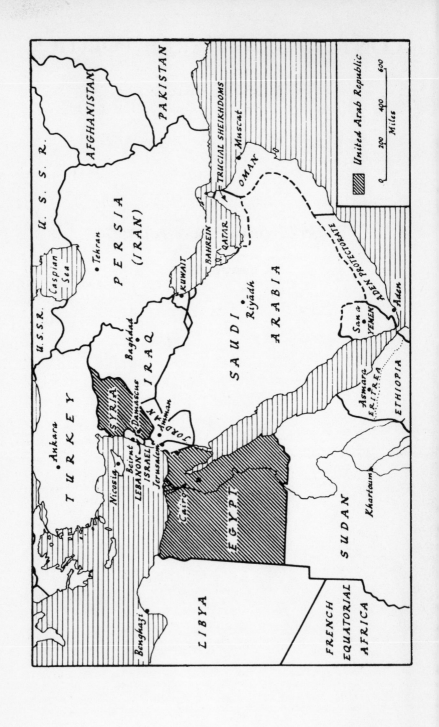

CONTEMPORARY ARAB POLITICS

A Concise History

by

George E. Kirk

FREDERICK A. PRAEGER, *Publishers*
NEW YORK, N. Y.

BOOKS THAT MATTER

First published in the United States of America in 1961
by Frederick A. Praeger, Inc., Publishers
64 University Place, New York 3, N. Y.

© 1961 by Frederick A. Praeger, Inc.

Library of Congress catalog card number 61-8176

CONTEMPORARY ARAB POLITICS is published in two editions:
A Praeger Paperback (PPS-34)
A clothbound edition

Manufactured in the United States of America

*In ages like the present one . . . violence and self-expression
and complication of motive have become so great that we need
a détente. It's the commonplace of the newspapers when they
talk of the cold war. But I believe this disengagement should
take place inside all of us. We need a simmering down of
human personality, of human achievement too if you like, in
order that we can start up again. Otherwise all will be lost in
the boiling over. . . .*

*Certainly violence will supervene many times. Violence
masked as greatness. But meanwhile if more and more people
simmer down we may eventually reach a safety point. On all
accounts . . . during this age, no more greatness. . . .*

*Or mediocrity claiming greatness. That makes an even
louder noise.*

(Angus Wilson, *The Middle Age of Mrs. Eliot.*)

CONTENTS

MAPS

INTRODUCTION

It has become increasingly evident during the past twelve years that the Arabic-speaking world is in a state of revolution, and that it has rejected not only the Western imperialism of the nineteenth century, but also the constitutionalism that seemed (theoretically, at least) to be the beneficent aspect of that same Western cultural influence of which imperialism has been assumed (perhaps too summarily) to be the harmful aspect. I say "theoretically" because, in fact, the ruling classes of the Arab countries, partly relying on "imperialist" support for themselves but also indulging their own self-willed appetites for power and material gain, had so abused these liberal constitutions that their abolition by the new revolutionary regimes has occasioned remarkably little regret on anyone's part.

Revolutions are the raw process of history, in which the skin and cosmetics of more orderly periods are stripped off and the tissues and nerves of a society laid bare.[1] The sight is sometimes one to turn a tender stomach. Violent deeds and still more violent words become the norm, as Thucydides once observed; and the dispassionate review of causes and events may become a luxury reserved for the historian belonging to a later generation or enjoying an exceptional degree of personal detachment.

I cannot pretend to possess that quality of detachment. Two earlier works of mine have been listed in a bibliography with the justified comment that "the author's point of view often shines through his factual narrative."[2] Personally, when I read a book, I like to know the author's point of view; reading a purely factual narrative can too often be like traveling through a valley of dry bones. The critic may well find that passages in this present book are prejudiced, overstated, tendentious. If these qualities provoke other writers to publish their own interpretations, and the reader is thus provided with a basis for comparison and for the exercise of his own judgment, I will have accomplished something that, at this point of historical perspective in the handling of a contemporary subject, can never be achieved with emasculated "objective" writing.

CONTEMPORARY ARAB POLITICS

A Concise History

CHAPTER 1

THE MYTH OF THE FOURTEENTH
MUSLIM CENTURY

A major study by Alfred Rosenberg,[1] dealing with what he called the "myth of the twentieth century," was one of the most important influences on the ideology of the emerging German national-socialist (Nazi) movement. Though it is not my intention to imply that contemporary Arab nationalism shares the vices of the German Nazis, I believe that Arab nationalism has also gradually evolved through its historic experience, whether real or imaginary, a myth of its own which I venture to call the "myth of the fourteenth Muslim century" (1883-1980 A.D.). By referring to it as a myth, I am not suggesting that it is wholly unhistoric.[2] But all historic events of importance take on, in the eyes of later generations, accretions which are not wholly historic or whose significance is more or less distorted to serve an ideology. Thus, Protestant England has or had its myth of the English "Reformation"; Whig England has or had its myth of the English Civil War and "Glorious Revolution"; the United States still cherishes its myth of the War of Independence or "Revolution"; and my generation in Britain has partly evolved a myth out of the Battle of Britain in 1940. Why, therefore, should Arab nationalism not have its myth of the fourteenth Muslim century?

In his pioneering narrative *The Arab Awakening,*[3] George Antonius portrayed the first modern Arab nationalists of nearly 100 years ago as Christian Arabs studying in Western schools like the Syrian Protestant College (which later became the American University of Beirut). But at about the same time, a Muslim "awakening" was taking place independently, as a few Muslims gradually realized that worldly power had in recent decades decisively passed from the Ottoman Empire to a pack of unbelieving "Franks" in Western Europe who were exploiting new technological developments like the steamship and the telegraph to extend their material power. This was a challenge, not only to the political security of the Muslim world but to the very roots of Muslim belief, for the extraordinary worldly success of Islam in conquering for itself within one century of its Prophet's death an empire greater in extent than the Roman Empire at its height had come to be regarded as an outward and visible sign of Allah's favor for his "chosen people." And though the controlling hands of the Muslim Empire had changed with the passing of the centuries—from Arab to Persian to Turk—those controlling hands were still Muslim, so the divine promise of worldly power to the Realm of Islam (Dar ul-Islam) was not brought into question. The empire had long been based on the principle of religion, not of nationality, and the newfangled nationalism of nineteenth-century Europe had not yet begun to infect Dar ul-Islam; so the pious Muslim, as late as the end of the eighteenth century, could paraphrase Browning's Pippa and say, "Allah's in his heaven; all's right with the Muslim world."

But in the nineteenth century, the impact of European imperialism was to disturb his comfortable repose. To quote Wilfred Cantwell Smith, whose recent study has given us a new depth of penetration in this field: "In Muslim conviction power comes from God, and yet here were the British empire, the Dutch empire, the French empire growing daily more powerful than Islamic society. . . . Islamic backwardness implies that something has gone wrong, not only with the Muslim's own development but with the governance of the universe."[4] The shock to accepted Muslim belief was as great as the shock of the Babylonian exile had been to conventional-minded Jews of the sixth century B.C.; but whereas the Babylonian exile drew out of the wounded side of Jewry prophets like Jeremiah and the Second Isaiah—who, out of this bitter experience, learned and taught new lessons, at a deeper moral and spiritual level, on the true relationship between God and His chosen people—Islam in its fourteenth century has thus far not produced its major prophet. It has produced only Gamal Abdel Nasser and Abdul Karim Qasim.

But this is not quite a fair comparison, and in any case it anticipates the course of events. At a much earlier stage of Islam's discomfiture under the impact of Western imperialism, it did produce a prophet of importance, Saiyid Jamal ud-Din al-Afghani (he died in 1897), who might be loosely compared with the Jewish minor prophet Nahum. Afghani, in his peregrinations between Istanbul and Cairo, was the first to manifest (in Cantwell Smith's words):

> . . . another developing aspect of modern Islamic consciousness: an explicit nostalgia for the departed earthly glory of pristine Islam. With his ebullient rhetoric and tireless repetition, Afghani fired audiences in one Muslim country after another to a reawakened consciousness of how they had once been mighty, but now were weak. This memory was not far below the surface, but it was below and was generally without delineation, a feeling rather than a picture of past greatness. His vivid evocations elicited a spirited response that has since

ramified. Indeed in addition to internal reform and external defense, this recalling of erstwhile Muslim grandeur has become a third dominant trait of modern Islam. . . .

Further, Afghani exhibited a partial appreciation of intellectualism and of Western values and particularly Western science and techniques. He saw the West as something primarily to be resisted, because it threatened Islam and the community, but secondly, in part to be imitated. He was vigorous in inciting his Muslim hearers to develop reason and technology, as the West is doing, *in order to be strong.*[5]

In a world dominated by power politics, it would clearly be unreasonable to chide a re-emergent society for wishing to be physically strong. But at the same time, it would be willful obscurantism not to recognize the intoxicating allure which the prospect of power holds for Muslim Arabs. Not only does it offer them, as it did the Zionists, a means of security against alien interference; but it is also, as the Promised Land was for the Zionists, the fulfillment of the Scripture, of Allah's assurance that Dar ul-Islam shall be supreme and that the unbelievers shall meekly pay it tribute. That is why Abdel Nasser's arms deal with the Soviet Union (temporarily disguised as Czechoslovakia) in September, 1955, immediately awakened such enthusiasm among the young Arab nationalists outside Egypt who had hitherto refrained from committing themselves to the Egyptian revolutionary movement. (They all had approved of the expulsion of Faruq, of course; but the quarrel between the young clique of Free Officers and that now-forgotten man, General Mohammed Nagib, had caused misgivings which were increased by Abdel Nasser's acceptance of conditions for the British withdrawal from the Suez Canal Zone and, above all, by his determined repression of the widespread Muslim Brotherhood when it made an attempt on his life.) This enthusiasm was not an expression

of pro-Communist, or even pro-Soviet, sentiment; it arose
from the realization that the Arab world was no longer dependent on the goodwill of the Western nations for the arms
which were the means for achieving power—that the Soviet
Union was now benevolently playing the role of fairy god-
father which the extremists of twenty years earlier had hoped
Nazi Germany would play (until they were disillusioned by
the Germans' desertion of Rashid Ali's *Putsch* in Iraq in
May, 1941).[6]

For the Arab nationalist, the final evidence that the West
was no friend of his cause—and had, indeed, betrayed his
cause—lay in the handling of the Palestine problem, from the
British Government's issuance of the Balfour Declaration in
1917 to President Truman's support of militant Zionism beginning in 1945 and extending to the armistice of 1949,
which established the state of Israel *de facto* behind lines
that have since acquired a certain permanence. It is impossible
to exaggerate the importance of the Palestine case in the drift
of Arab nationalism to its present extremes; and yet, it would
be unreal to pretend that this is the only grievance, that the
relations between Arab nationalists and the West would be
entirely harmonious if it were not for the Zionist interlopers.
Another major charge of Arab nationalism against the West
concerns the so-called "broken promises" of which Britain
is alleged to have been guilty in her relations with the Arabs
during and after World War I. And just as, in the Palestine
issue, there has grown around the core of genuine grievance
(Western partiality for the Zionists) a luxuriant crop of popular Arab mythology designed to explain away the ignominious
Arab defeat,[7] so the failure of the Arabs to achieve their independence after World War I, which was due partly to Western
"imperialism" but also to their own leaders' double-dealing
and ineptitude in negotiating with the Western powers, has

been explained away by the myth of "broken promises," which
has also found a ready echo in those Western circles that are
ready to think the worst of their fellow Westerners.[8]

Nor do the grievances or the mythology stop with World
War I. The shifting of responsibility for Arab or Muslim
weakness at the time of the Western impact has been carried
back even further than the rise of the Ottoman Empire and
the thirteenth-century Mongol invasions (a favorite whipping
boy for some) to the Crusades, which Abdel Nasser has described as "the beginning of the dark ages in our country."
Before that there was the dazzling luster of the Muslim
"golden age"; but here again, one may find a young Arab
nationalist who avers that this "golden age" was curtailed by
"the Arab conquests and expansion; the extension of the Arab
domain over so many different peoples, which led to the loss
of its own harmony, its cohesion, and, ultimately, of its independence. Foreign intellectual trends infiltrated and diluted
the Arab spirit inspired and led by Islam."[10] Conversely, some
of the most enthusiastic Arab nationalists have not allowed
even the rise of Islam and the expansion of the Arabs beyond
the borders of their arid peninsula to delimit the range of their
mythologizing. A former Director General of Education in
Iraq (significantly, during the period of the Nazi heyday in
Germany) urged upon Baghdad schoolteachers in 1939:

> We have up to now neglected a most vital aspect of our
> glorious history; we have made it start at the prophetic mes-
> sage, and this is a period of less than fourteen centuries. In
> reality, however, the history of our illustrious Arab nation
> extends over thousands of years, and goes back to the time
> when the peoples of Europe lived in forests and over
> marshes, in caves and in the interstices of the rock; at that
> time our own ancestors used to set up banks, sculpt statues,
> and lay down canons and codes of law; they invented then

the first principles of medicine, geometry, astronomy, the
alphabet, and the numerals. . . . We find that everything
makes us lift our heads high when we consider the histories
of the Semitic empires formed in the Fertile Crescent. . . .
We have the right to glory in them and to honour their
exploits, just as we have the right to cherish and exalt the
glories of Nabuchadnezzar, Hammurabi, Sargon, Rameses,
Tutankhamen, in the same way that we glory and take
pride in . . . Hārūn ar-Rashīd . . .[11]

This cannot be dismissed as an isolated example of mega-
lomania, for in 1957 a booklet issued by the Federation of
Kuwaiti Student Missions in Egypt asserted: "Thousands of
years ago, successive waves of Arabs [*sic*] moved from the
Peninsula to the Fertile Crescent and the Nile Valley."[12] And
at the 1960 Conference of the Middle East Institute, the
former Secretary-General of the Arab League advanced these
same Arab claims not only to Hammurabi, Sargon, and
Thothmes, but to Jesus of Nazareth as well.[13]

Like Pan-Germanism, Pan-Arabism in its extreme mani-
festations has developed a mystique of *Blut und Erde* which
makes it seek to appropriate all preceding civilizations that
have arisen and flourished on the "sacred" soil of the "fatherland." And whereas the prevailing tone of Arab nationalist
thinking twenty-five years ago seemed to be liberal and ideal-
istic as exemplified by men like Taha Husain, Constantin
Zuraiq, and Charles Malik,[14] the upsurge of "radical nationalism"[15] in the last decade has compelled such men into either
tacit acquiescence or cultural exile. It is as if, in one generation, the "wave of the future" had swept this politically im-
mature people along from the inspirations of a Hegel to the
mystagogy of an Alfred Rosenberg. And just as, quite apart
from the changes and chances of historical fortune, some of
the national predispositions that gave Adolf Hitler his oppor-

tunity can with hindsight be discerned in the ill-digested German *Aufklärung,* if not in the Lutheran Reformation,[16] so can some of the temperamental excesses which have given rise to the rancorous propaganda-spouting dictatorships of the contemporary Arab world be seen foreshadowed in the uncertain "Arab awakening" described by George Antonius, if not in the Arabic "golden age" itself.[17]

It is my aim in the following chapters to illustrate and enlarge on these judgments expressed here.

CHAPTER 2

THE SAPPING OF THE SEVEN PILLARS

World War II, with its heavy concentration of the forces of the British Commonwealth and its allies in the Middle East, put the political evolution of that region into temporary cold storage for five years. Those who were responsible for advising on British policy—notably the unassuming and underrated Brigadier (later Sir) Iltyd Clayton, Adviser on Arab Affairs to the Minister Resident in the Middle East—fully realized how temporary this suspension of the normal political fervor in the Arab world must be; and the encouragement which such men gave behind the scenes to the formation of the League of Arab States, for example, was intended as a means of turning off the British-induced refrigeration gradually, in the hope that the more conservative forces within Arab nationalism might themselves thereafter keep the nationalist "bouillon" suitably chilled.[1] Clayton reckoned among these conservative forces not only such obvious figures as Nuri as-Sa'id of Iraq and the Amir Abdullah of Transjordan, but also his personal friend Sa'dullah Jābiri (Prime Minister of Syria until his death in 1946) and probably Mahmud Fahmi an-Nuqrashi in Egypt.[2] Observant but never aggressive, Clayton (who was a Roman Catholic) remained aware, throughout

21

the spurious Anglo-Soviet honeymoon of 1941-45, of the
challenge which Soviet policy was likely to present to British
interests in the postwar Middle East, and his advice probably
had something to do with the return to Iran in 1943 of Saiyid
Ziya ud-Din Tabataba'i in an attempt to organize opposition
to the Soviet-supported Tudeh Party, which then seemed to be
carrying all before it in Iran.[3]

But it was hardly possible that anyone responsible for
the shaping of British policy could have foreseen the immedi-
acy and crudity of the Soviet cold-war offensive against Iran
and Turkey less than six months after the end of World War
II; as a result, the British Government was even more un-
willing than it might otherwise have been to reduce its strategic holdings in the region in response to nationalist pressure.
Furthermore, the coming to power of the Labour Party in
Britain undoubtedly caused Middle Eastern nationalists, notably in Egypt, to hope that the new incumbents in West-
minster would be softer in yielding to nationalist pressure than
a government led by Winston Churchill;[4] and as Walter Z.
Laqueur has shown, Communists and fellow travelers were
already organized in the Middle East to add their agitation to
that of the bourgeois nationalists for an immediate end to
"imperialism." The unilateral withdrawal of the United States
forces from Iran three months before the date determined for
the final withdrawal of the foreign troops from that country
undoubtedly encouraged Stalin and his fellow conspirators
to think that they could easily break down the nerve of the
single-handed and enfeebled British; it was only the stubborn
opposition of one man, Ernest Bevin, that held the line of
the Elburz range during the winter of 1945-46, until the education of the U.S. State Department was complete and Ambassador George V. Allen could take his place in organizing
Iranian resistance to the Soviet bully.[5]

But it was the impatient Zionists, limited in their vision, who played a large part in wrecking the chances for keeping postwar Middle Eastern nationalism at a relatively moderate level. With that myopic disregard for the geographical context of their political aspirations which had characterized them from the beginning, the Zionists' skillful combination of humanitarian appeal, political intrigue, deceptive propaganda, occasional bribery, and some terrorist acts from 1945 through 1947 not only raised Palestine to fever pitch, but systematically undermined the already shaken British prestige throughout the region[6] at a time when no other power—and least of all the United States—was ready to substitute its authority in the Middle East for that of the declining British. Thus the Zionists, and their important friends like President Truman, contributed greatly to the creation in the Middle East of that power vacuum which most Western observers came to recognize as an apt description of its situation. The decline of British authority in the region in the postwar period was, of course, inevitable in any case; and it was soon recognized that the achievement of independence by India and Pakistan in 1947 was an important factor in encouraging the Iranian nationalist attack on the Anglo-Iranian Oil Company three years later. But without the systematic and successful Zionist flouting of British authority in Palestine, the transition might have been more gradual, the substitution of some other authority (preferably that of the United States) more coherently planned.

As it was, the Palestine War of 1948—that crazy combination of Zionist and Arab intransigence, Bevin's stubbornness at odds with his colleagues' general failure of nerves,[7] United States and United Nations irresponsibility and sheer ignorance—constituted, far more than did World War II, the great divide of contemporary Middle Eastern history. Its reve-

lation of incompetence and disunity in the League of Arab
States disrupted the pattern of Arab conservative rule under
which Clayton had hoped that the League might develop in
an evolutionary fashion. In Egypt, Prime Minister Nuqrashi
was murdered by the Muslim Brotherhood during the final
rout of the Egyptian Army from Palestine (December, 1948);
in Syria, the "old oligarchs"[8] of the National Bloc Party were
swept aside by the first of the military *coups d'état* of 1949;[9]
and in Iraq, the "balloon had gone up" in *advance* of the Palestine War, when the extreme nationalists and Communists
jointly wrecked the proposed new Anglo-Iraqi treaty signed at
Portsmouth, England, in January, 1948.[10] The murder of King
Abdullah of Jordan in July, 1951, by a group of Palestinian
Arab conspirators located in Cairo and enjoying the protection
of the Egyptian Government was a delayed phenomenon of
the same process.

The deflating of the "old oligarchs" in Syria led to greatly
increased influence by the younger "progressives," organized
in the Ba'th (Resurrectionist) Party—whose leaders (Salah
ud-Din Bitar and Michel Aflaq) were schoolteachers who had
acquired left-wing notions during a brief prewar sojourn at
the Sorbonne—or in the Arab Socialist Party of Akram Hawrani. Hawrani and the eventual victor in the three Syrian
coups d'état of 1949, Colonel Adib Shishakli, both hailed from
the traditionally conservative city of Hama in central Syria.
Shishakli belonged to one of the four or five leading families
of Hama and gave the impression of being a man whose sense
of order and authority was greater than his intelligence; he
was one of nature's fascists, to put it in a rather unkindly
way, and he had indeed been associated with the Syrian National Party (Hizb al-Qawmi as-Suri), whose prewar founder,
Antun Sa'ada (sentenced to death by a drumhead court-martial
in Lebanon after an attempted *coup* in 1949) had injected the

party with a strong dose of the *Führerprinzip*. Hawrani, on
the other hand, came from a family of lower social standing,
had a rat-like intelligence and cunning, and probably hoped
to be the political "gray eminence" directing the policy of the
slower-witted Shishakli.[11] But after the latter's second *coup*
in December, 1951, when he stripped away the constitutional
trappings and exposed himself boldly as a military dictator
(though he still retained the prop of General Fawzi Silu mas-
querading as the head of state, Syria's version of Victor Em-
manuel III), it was only a matter of months before Hawrani
found Shishakli no longer responsive to his suggestions for a
drastic land reform at the expense of the owners of the great
latifundia of the Hama district; instead, Shishakli followed a
conservative and specifically anti-Communist policy. There
were some who suggested that the attentions of the U.S. Embassy were responsible for this change, and I remember a
woman member of the British community at a party in Damascus in December, 1952, describing the dictator as a
"poppet." At the end of that year, Shishakli unearthed a conspiracy against him in the planning stage, and the three malcontents—Hawrani, Aflaq, and Bitar—fled across the frontier
to Beirut. There, three months later, when I asked the two
Ba'this what the difference was between their party and
Akram Hawrani's Arab Socialist Party, they assured me that
the Ba'th had evolved a set of logically thought-out principles,
whereas Hawrani was a pure opportunist. But this did not prevent them from joining forces with Hawrani after their return
to Syria and the downfall of the now isolated Shishakli in
February, 1954. With Shishakli's eclipse, the reunited left—the
Ba'th Socialist Party, as it now called itself—faced the older
bourgeois parties, the National Party located in Damascus
and the People's Party located in Aleppo. The story of how
the Ba'th succeeded in rising above its slender numerical base

in the Syrian Parliament and, by a series of staged conspiracy trials and by progressive intimidation of the moderates, establishing itself as the dominant political force remains to be treated in a later section of this study.[12]

While the Palestine War was the grand climacteric for the "old oligarchs" of Syria, its effect in Egypt, though ultimately decisive, was less immediate. It is true—as the memoirs of Mohammed Nagib, Gamal Abdel Nasser, Anwar as-Sadat, and others have shown—that it was that war which brought the discontented young officers together, gave them a sense of national and professional humiliation, and (Middle Eastern nature being what it is) led them to *project* their sense of failure upon the fat and frivolous Faruq and the "establishment," whose dishonesty and treachery they had come to consider as the sole cause of the military defeat.[13] But for the Egyptians the Palestine War was, in fact, merely a side show; their major objective was to rid the Nile Valley finally of the British. It was the British, not the Zionists, who were Egypt's prime enemy,[14] and the Egyptian establishment was able to survive the murder of Prime Minister Nuqrashi in 1949 and restore some kind of order only through its ruthless suppression of the Muslim Brotherhood. The return to power of the Wafd, as a result of the election of 1950, merely meant the supremacy of a more disreputable alternative establishment, dominated by the Wafdist Secretary-General and Minister of the Interior, Fu'ad Sirag ud-Din; the multimillionaire Ahmad 'Abbud; and Faruq's Lebanese private secretary, Karim Thabit.[15] The Wafd's denunciation of the Anglo-Egyptian Treaty and the Sudan Condominium, and its plunge into guerrilla warfare against the British in the Suez Canal Zone (in autumn, 1951) were highly popular moves, besides being necessary to divert attention from the irresponsible private speculations in cotton practiced by the

Wafdist leaders during the Korean War scare. The Egyptian
Army was officially kept out of the guerrilla activities because
the British held positions along its lines of communication between the Delta and its forward positions near the Israeli
border; and while some of the young officer malcontents did
join the guerrillas (with no very spectacular results), they had
not yet begun to take an independent line:

> At the time the Free Officers' tracts supported the Wafd,
> and without shutting their eyes to the domestic administra-
> tion of Nahas's government, Nasser and his friends backed
> what—along with the masses—they called the patriotic
> struggle.
>
> They reacted as Wafdist sympathizers to the burning
> of Cairo and the Ministry's dismissal, as can be seen from
> a tract they put out early in March, 1952. In it the Officers
> denounced Neguib el Hilali's talk of "purging" the country
> before freeing it of the [British] occupier. This was exactly
> the same as the Wafd's attitude. . . . Also on the next day
> Nasser went to see Ahmed Abul Fath, editor-in-chief of the
> daily El Misri and a Wafd representative, to inform him that
> he and his group were preparing to take action, and offering
> to coordinate their activities with the Wafd's. . . .[16]

There are other passages that throw a significant light on
the state of mind of the Free Officers before their seizure of
power in 1952. We learn that at one time prominent members
of the group like Salāh Sālim or Anwar as-Sadat had proposed that each of the dozen leading conspirators should
undertake the murder of one of the most harmful personalities
of the Faruq regime, or that the British Embassy should be
dynamited.[17] And Anwar as-Sadat solemnly recounts how,
during the guerrilla actions in the Suez Canal Zone against
the British in December, 1951, he and his fellow conspirators
in Sinai were sent "a powerful mine which we planned to give

as a Christmas present to the first British ship which passed
through the Canal. We had not expected anything so large,
for it was a monstrous affair, contained in four cases. . . . In
fact, the mine was never exploded. It is still carefully hidden
away somewhere in Egypt, where the Free Officers determined
that it should remain as long as there was a British soldier in
the Canal Zone."[18]

CHAPTER 3

THE FREE OFFICERS
LOSE THEIR FREEDOM

For the first two and a half years after their expulsion of Faruq and seizure of power in July, 1952, the Egyptian Free Officers had a generally favorable world press, except in the U.S.S.R.; the Communists had selected the Wafd Party as the party of bourgeois nationalism because they calculated, first, that it could get rid of the British through its intransigence and, second, that it would pave the way eventually for Communism through its incompetence and corruption.[1] In some American circles, approval of the reforms undertaken by the new military regime was expressed in terms bordering on adulation. Jefferson Caffery, the U.S. Ambassador to Egypt from 1949 to 1955, had been in favor of recognizing Faruq as King of the Sudan and had had talks with the palace clique until very shortly before the revolution;[2] but he now adopted the military junta as his "boys" and is reported to have said, "They have done more for Egypt in two years than all their predecessors put together did before them."[3] In the view of the British Ambassador in Cairo, American policy:

. . . seemed to be conditioned by a belief that Egypt was still the victim of British "colonialism," and as such deserving of

29

American sympathy. It also appeared to be influenced by a desire to reach a quick solution almost at any cost and by a pathetic belief that, once agreement was reached, all would be well. These considerations, combined with a horror of unpopularity and fear of losing their influence with the new regime, particularly on the part of the United States Embassy in Cairo and also an apparent disinclination by the United States Government to take second place even in an area where primary responsibility was not theirs, resulted in the Americans, at least locally, withholding the wholehearted support which their partner in NATO had the right to expect. . . . Inevitably the Egyptians exploited the equivocal American attitude.[4]

Objectively, the new Egyptian regime's record in autumn, 1954, was a favorable one. In spite of its increasing smothering of opposition by "Gestapo methods," it seemed "free of some of the vices of the Wafd and showed no signs as yet of those wider ambitions of empire which Colonel Nasser was later to proclaim and pursue."[5] The regime had undertaken land reforms which, if they could not cure Egypt's urgent problem of rural overpopulation, were at least an earnest of its good intentions and apparent readiness to be assisted in grappling with this problem.[6] Its leaders had abandoned the foolish assertion of their predecessors, from Nuqrashi to the Wafd, that the people of the Sudan unanimously desired to be united with Egypt,[7] and had reached an agreement with the British in February, 1953, to make Sudanese self-determination a reality. The Sudanese general election of November, 1953, which gave a comfortable majority to the party hitherto regarded as pro-Egyptian, seemed to be the reward of Nagib's common sense. In the most difficult matter of all, that of the Suez Canal base, the regime had (after a long period of sometimes acrimonious, often suspended negotiation) compromised with the British by conceding that for a period of seven years the British might reoccupy the base in the event of an aggression from outside the Middle East against a member state of the Arab League *or against Turkey*. This agreement of October, 1954, which secured a pledge by the British to withdraw their forces within twenty-one months, was presented to the Egyptian public as a great victory and was celebrated by the issue of a commemorative postage stamp; and during the period between the signing of the agreement and its ratification, spokesmen of the regime from Abdel Nasser downward gave such assurances as the following one of their identification with the West: "There seems no doubt that Egypt today holds in all respects to the side of the West. Her culture, her commerce, and her economic life are bound to the West. Ideologically, she is definitely opposed to Communism. Militarily, she considers that the only danger capable of threatening the Middle East is a Soviet invasion."[8]

But this apparent *rapprochement* with the West had the disadvantage of giving a handle to all the opponents of the regime: the Communists; the Muslim Brotherhood; the Wafdist supporters, who had been driven underground by repression but certainly not destroyed; the adherents of General Nagib, who had been forced into the background in the obscure struggle of March-April, 1954, and now tried to reassert himself by opposing the agreement with Britain.[9] There may have been dissension among the inner ranks of the Officers themselves, though there is no definite evidence of this; but certainly the shots fired at Abdel Nasser by a member of the Muslim Brotherhood at Alexandria on October 26, 1954, demonstrated that the basis of the regime's popular support had become dangerously weak. The regime's reaction was a characteristic one. Members of the Brotherhood were arrested, confessions were extracted by beatings in the tra-

ditional Egyptian manner,[10] and the assailant and five other
leading members of the organization were hanged. But at the
same time, the regime's policy was being modified in a more
popular—that is to say, nationalist—direction.

There were other reasons for this, besides the need to
restore the internal prestige of the regime. John Foster Dulles,
during his orientation tour of the Middle East shortly after
becoming Secretary of State in the spring of 1953, had reported that he had found the countries of the "northern tier"
of the region the ones most aware of the threat to their independence coming from the U.S.S.R. That Turkey and Pakistan should be ready to accept military aid from the United
States was not a matter of immediate concern to Egypt, still
preoccupied with her efforts to secure the withdrawal of
British troops from the Suez Canal Zone; but when the Iraqi
Government, led by Nuri as-Sa'id, showed a similar readiness
to accept arms from the United States early in 1954, this
action brought upon it a violent attack from the Egyptian
propaganda machine.[11] Apologists for the Cairo regime (notably those well-meaning "liberals" supplying the *Economist,
Observer,* and *Manchester Guardian* with pabulum for intellectual chiding of the British Government) assured us that
this outbreak was occasioned only by the desire to keep the
Arab League solid against defense arrangements with the West
until the British evacuation was secured. Just get that out of
the way, spokesmen like Tom Little[12] assured us, and you will
see how accommodating Nasser will be: "He told me so himself!"

However, the personality of Iraq's elder statesman, Nuri
as-Sa'id, and the great increase of revenue which Iraq was
now receiving as royalties from the Iraq Petroleum Company
promised to give that country a degree of independence which
could hardly be harmonized with Egypt's pre-eminence in the

Arab League—a position accorded to Egypt at the League's inception and one that it was a matter of prestige for the military regime to maintain. Consequently, when Nuri talked of replacing the Anglo-Iraqi Treaty of 1930 (now approaching its expiration date) with a regional defense agreement of the kind provided by Article 51 of the United Nations Charter,[13] he made little impression on Abdel Nasser at their meeting in September, 1954; and when the Arab League held its autumn conference in Cairo in December, after the suppression of the Muslim Brotherhood, Nasser insisted that there must be no contracting of new alliances outside the Arab League Security Pact, which had been originally devised, in part, to preserve Egypt's pre-eminence within the League.[14] It might be that after a year or so of internal indoctrination and external bargaining, Egypt would be ready to enter some sort of defense pact with the West on terms favorable to herself, in which case the rest of the Arab League would be directed to conform; but until that time, no initiative from any of Egypt's satellites would be tolerated.

However, this was not a policy acceptable to the Iraqi elder statesman, who had been the chief personal aide to the Amir Faisal in 1919, when Egypt's self-appointed young rulers of 1954 were still making mudpies in some village street. Nor was the seemingly unending delay acceptable to the Turkish Prime Minister, Menderes, who had also placed a too optimistic interpretation upon the conclusion of the Anglo-Egyptian agreement and had been pressing for an invitation to visit Abdel Nasser as a preliminary to a regional defense agreement. The Egyptians had suggested a more gradual approach, with visits to Egypt by the Mayors of Ankara and Istanbul to get Egyptian public opinion used to the idea of more friendly relations with Turkey; and a fulsome preface to an official pamphlet on this subject had appeared under Nasser's own name. But after a Turkish press delegation to Egypt in December, 1954, had been fobbed off with an unfriendly harangue from Salāh Sālim and glib talk from the Egyptian Foreign Minister about "cultural relations in the fields of radio, art, the theater, tourism, and university contacts,"[15] Menderes decided that there was nothing to be expected from Egypt and went ahead with his planned visit to Iraq in January, 1955.

The Baghdad correspondents of the leading U.S. and British newspapers agreed that, in view of Egypt's opposition, nothing in the nature of a pact between Turkey and Iraq was immediately likely; but the joint communiqué issued at the end of the two statesmen's meeting on January 12 announced that the two governments had "decided to conclude a treaty as soon as possible." Two days later, the Egyptian Government organ, al-Gumhurīya—controlled by Anwar as-Sadat, who counted as one of the most extreme members of the military junta—declared that the Iraqi Government's action was "in complete contradiction with the spirit of the Arab League charter and collective pact"[16] and alleged that Turkey had concluded a nonaggression pact with Israel, thus insinuating that Iraq was indirectly involved with the enemy of all true Arabs. The Egyptian Government convened an extraordinary meeting of the Prime Ministers of the Arab states with a view to isolating Nuri and compelling him to abandon the proposed pact with Turkey. At the same time, the Egyptian military attaché in Baghdad was conducting an intrigue to arouse popular opposition to the Iraqi Government; but the attempt was a failure, and Nuri remained firmly in the saddle.[17]

It was urgent that something be done to repair this new blow to Egyptian prestige, still suffering from the repercussions in other Arab countries of the hanging of the six members of the Muslim Brotherhood. Already, in December, 1954, a trial had opened in Cairo of a group of thirteen alleged Israeli agents accused of espionage and attempted fire-raising with a view to arousing public alarm. On January 27, 1955, two of the accused were sentenced to death and six others to terms of imprisonment (the alleged leader of those arrested had committed suicide in prison a month earlier), and four days later the two death sentences were carried out. *The Times* remarked in a leading article on February 4 that "it was a mistake to ignore the many representations, made by some of. Egypt's best friends [including the U.S. State Department] which urged the commutation of the death sentences [imposed for] . . . sabotage too amateurish to be taken seriously"; and the impression was left that the severity was a political device intended to balance the draconic treatment of the Muslim Brotherhood. Whatever its effect in Egypt, it had the further effect (doubtless unforeseen by Cairo) of bringing the veteran David Ben-Gurion out of his retirement in a *kibbutz,* to which he had withdrawn after the drastic Israeli reprisals against Arab raiders across the armistice lines (culminating in the Israeli destruction of the Jordanian villages of Qibya and Nahalin in 1953 and' 1954) had brought upon Israel the strong condemnation of the United Nations. On February 17, 1955, Ben-Gurion once again became Defense Minister of Israel, and eleven days later the Israeli forces launched a surprise attack on the Egyptian-occupied town of Gaza, killing some forty Egyptian soldiers and giving the Palestine Arab refugees of the crowded Gaza strip an object lesson in the inability of the Egyptian Army to defend them.

It is remarkable that two such perspicacious analysts of the Middle East crisis as Guy Wint and Peter Calvocoressi should have chronicled the Gaza raid as "one of the most fateful dates in Middle East history"[18] without even mentioning the Egyptian hanging of the two Israeli "spies" as an aggravating cause;

but these two writers were surveying the recent past with the astigmatism which the Suez crisis induced in all good "liberals" and "progressives," some of whom conveniently forgot that they had been aiding and abetting Israel and Zionism in fair weather and foul all their lives. An editorial in *The Times* of March 2, 1955, had been more comprehending when it remarked:

> Allowance must be made for the exasperation caused in Israel by espionage, raiding, and sabotage directed from the Gaza enclave (for which Egypt has been censured by the Armistice Commission), as well as by more open manifestations by the Egyptian Government of implacable hostility. The continued detention of the freighter *Bat Galim;* the interference with Israel-bound traffic in the Suez Canal;[19] the execution of two of the Jewish defendants in the Cairo spy-trial—all these have brought Israeli resentment against Egypt to fever-heat.

Furthermore, the correspondent of *The Times* in Israeli Jerusalem reported on March 5:

> It is believed that the activities in Israel of a well-trained band of spies and saboteurs, which had been particularly active the week before, set off an operation that had been under consideration for some time. The United Nations observers themselves had evidence from a captured Arab saboteur to the effect that Arabs in the Gaza strip were being trained by a military organization to carry out espionage and sabotage in Israel.

But when General Burns passed on these suspicions, "the position of the Egyptian authorities was that persons committing murders and sabotage were being inspired, paid, and equipped by political elements in Egypt inimical to the Government and desirous of aggravating the border situation."[20] Six months later, however, Cairo Radio was to boast of the patriotic exploits of these same *fedayeen*.

The Gaza raid seriously compromised the precarious prestige of the Egyptian Army and of the military regime itself; and, as two sympathetic writers have since commented, "Arms became an urgent necessity for Nasser if he was to retain the loyalty of his Free Officers and the army upon whom his control of Egypt rested."[21] He could have had arms from the United States on the same terms as did Iraq—that is, an agreement that they would not be used for aggressive purposes—but it was necessary to make the army and the public think (even if Nasser himself had a healthy respect for Israel's ability and readiness to return blow for blow) that armaments were being accumulated for a victorious "second round" against the Israelis; and accordingly, in July, the Egyptian Foreign Minister was reported to have told Mr. Dulles that "Egypt has not asked the United States for a grant of arms because she does not want to accept the strings and interference which . . . go with the United States military aid programs."[22]

Until this time, neither the United States nor the British Government, in the attempts of each to create some kind of regional defense organization for the Middle East, seems to have paid much heed to the signs of a revival of Soviet interest in the area following Stalin's death.[23] Indeed, the spring of 1955, with the moves toward holding a summit conference at Geneva, was a period in which Western optimists were indulging the hope that the cold war might at last be adjudicated as a "draw," without loss of dignity to either side. It is, of course, impossible to know to what extent the Soviet planners for the Middle East were provoked by Dulles' "northern tier" policy, which found expression in the Turko-Iraqi pact signed in February, 1955;[24] or (as the British opposition were to charge afterward, in their frustration at being defeated again in the

1955 election) by Britain's adherence to the Baghdad Pact at
the end of March.[25] It is, indeed, possible that the Russians
discerned that the British move was not welcomed in Washington,[26] and may have decided that the time was ripe for
exploitation. We must recall in this connection that Abdel
Nasser's attendance at the Bandung Conference in April, 1955,
was his first journey outside the limited horizons of Egypt, the
Sudan, and that part of Palestine temporarily occupied by
the Egyptian Army during the war of 1948. The Egyptian
press had duly played up Egypt's budding leader (his prestige
urgently in need of refurbishing from the tarnish caused by
the Baghdad Pact and the Gaza raid) as one of the "big
three" of the conference, along with Chou En-lai and Pandit
Nehru. And who is to assess the effect which this international
publicity had upon the burgeoning ego of the once-modest
bikbashi from the narrow confines of upper Egypt, between
those sterile cliffs that hem in both the Nile Valley and the
minds of its inhabitants? "The Bandung Conference showed
President Abdel Nasser all the advantages he could derive from
a 'neutralist' policy";[27] but at the same time he was about to
begin to surrender his freedom of maneuver.

The defiant announcement of the Egyptian-Soviet arms
deal at the end of September, 1955, thinly disguised as a commercial transaction with Czechoslovakia, immediately made
Nasser for the first time the darling of all the young nationalists
of the eastern Arab world. At last he had achieved what
Rashid Ali and the Mufti of Jerusalem had failed to achieve
with Nazi Germany in 1940-41[28]—a rewarding alliance with
a great power as a counterbalance to the West's lack of support for Arab aims. The fact that this opportunistic transaction[29] was made with the power responsible during thirty-odd
years for the repression of more than 20 million Muslims in
Turkestan caused no more moral compunction than Arab

extremism's previous intrigue with the men who were sending millions of European Jews to the gas chambers.

The U.S. State Department, alarmed by the sudden turn of Egyptian policy, hastily sent Ambassador George V. Allen (who had been its successful troubleshooter during the Soviet cold war against Iran in 1946-47) to represent to Abdel Nasser the risks he was incurring. Here is the dictator's own account of these proceedings, as he gave it to an Egyptian crowd some nine months later:

> I found that dispatches from Washington and news agencies were reporting: Mr. Allen has a warning for Egypt; Mr. Allen carried a threat to Egypt, a threat to sever this, that, and the other.
>
> Afterward, an American official contacted me and sought a special interview. He said that he regretted very much the state of the relations between the U.S.A. and Egypt. He also said: Allen has a strong note from the U.S. Government which might injure Egyptian national feeling and prestige. I assure you that this note will have no effect because we shall be able to undo its effect. I advise you to accept this message.
>
> I asked him what the insult to Egyptian national feeling and prestige was about.
>
> He said: It is a message from Mr. Dulles which is strongly worded. We are astonished how it came to be sent. We ask you to have cool nerves. You have always had cool nerves. Accept this message with cool nerves.
>
> I told him: How can I accept a message which contains a threat or injury to Egyptian dignity?
>
> He said that no practical outcome would result from this message and guaranteed this. He said: This written message will injure Egyptian dignity in words only, not in effect.
>
> I told him: Look, I am not a professional Premier. I

am a Premier of a revolution. . . . If your representative
comes to the office and says something unpleasant, I shall
dismiss him.

I shall proclaim to the Egyptian people that you wanted
to disparage their grandeur and dignity. We shall all fight
until the last drop of our blood. I myself shall fight for the
grandeur and dignity of Egypt to the last drop of my blood,
because these are the principles for which I have risen up. . . .
You may threaten to withhold aid. . . . I would come out
and declare that the aid was withheld. I shall make public
whatever else you threaten. And I would like you to know
that we have not taken any lessons in diplomacy and politics.
We are simply a group of people who started a revolution
and who seek to realize the aims of this revolution. . . .

He then came again and told me that he had told this
to Mr. Allen, and that Mr. Allen was wondering whether
he would be dismissed when he came to convey the message
to me and also whether Mr. Dulles would dismiss him if
he went back without conveying this message. What would
happen? I told him: I do not know. I only know one thing—
if he comes to convey this message to me I will dismiss him.
Whether Dulles dismisses him or not is [another] matter.

Then Mr. Allen came and did not open his mouth at
all. He sat and listened to the Egyptian point of view, and
briefly advanced the American viewpoint.

This is the hullabaloo about the arms and the arms deal.
The others were threatening and talking. Why did I say all
this? I said it while feeling fully confident. I said it, feeling
strong. Why? Because I felt that this entire people—23
million of them—would struggle to the last drop of their
blood for the grandeur which has been achieved and for independence. Yes, this whole nation.[30]

The Egyptian revolutionary government had already
adopted a project submitted to it by an Egyptian engineer (of
Greek origin) for the construction of a High Dam above

Aswan—a grandiose concept for increasing the Egyptian crop area by one-third and providing hydroelectric power at a total cost of $1.3 billion. It was considered an advantage to concentrate on a dam located solely in Egyptian territory, instead of a series of dams located in both Egypt and the Sudan[31] (now moving toward independence), though some 60,000 Sudanese would be displaced by the artificial lake formed behind the completed dam. The Sudan Government was anxious for a revision of the Nile Waters Agreement of 1929, which had been concluded between Egypt and Britain at a time when the Sudanese had no control over their affairs and was considered to be prejudicial to Sudanese interests. But when discussions were begun near the end of 1954, the Egyptian representatives were at first unwilling to present their High Dam project to the Sudanese,[32] and subsequent exchanges of views were acrimonious and unproductive. It was this failure of Egypt and the Sudan to come to terms on the division of water between them that caused the International Bank for Reconstruction and Development to move cautiously with respect to the High Dam project;[33] but after the Soviet Government announced in October, 1955, its readiness to help finance the dam, the United States and British Governments together offered $70 million, with the International Bank contributing a further $200 million, for the first stage of the work, "with the understanding that accomplishment of the project as a whole would require a satisfactory resolution of the question of Nile water rights" with the Sudan.[34] Other guarantees asked from the Egyptians were that they "would give the dam priority over other projects, that contracts would be awarded on a competitive basis, and that aid from Communist sources would be refused."[35] However, Abdel Nasser protested that these conditions were prejudicial to Egypt's sovereignty, that they were less favorable than the terms on which Israel had obtained

American loans, that they represented "a trick and a very major act of deception," and that the intent behind them was "economic domination and despotism." He went on: "If they wanted to offer this aid they should offer it in a memorandum free of any passage indicating that they would dominate our policy or sovereignty or economy and any passages representing domination over Egypt's independence."[36] Meanwhile, the Egyptian public and the world were fed with periodic rumors from the controlled Egyptian press that the Russians had come forward with a better offer—an offer that never took concrete form, however, even after Shepilov (by this time, Soviet Foreign Minister for a brief tenure before falling from favor in Moscow) had visited Cairo in June, 1956, to receive the plaudits of the crowds and assist (in spirit, at least) at the withdrawal of the last British troops from the Canal Zone in fulfillment of the agreement of 1954. The U.S. financial year was drawing to a close, and the State Department was reported to have warned Cairo that "the United States has not withdrawn the offer of help, but it will require a new appropriation by Congress."[37]

By early July, Nasser had apparently realized that no firm bid was forthcoming from Moscow, and he instructed his Ambassador to Washington that he should accept the Western offer. "It is now up to the West," the Ambassador told journalists. But on July 19, according to Sir Anthony Eden, "for reasons connected with the Senate's attitude to foreign aid and the critical climate towards neutralism then prevalent in Washington,[38] Mr. Dulles felt obliged to tell the Egyptian Ambassador that the deal was off." Eden added that his government was "informed but not consulted and so had no prior opportunity for criticism or comment. . . . We were sorry that the matter was carried through so abruptly, because it gave our two countries no chance to concert either timing or

methods, though these were quite as important as the substance. I would have preferred to play this long and not to have
forced the issue."[39] For Dulles, on the other hand, according
to his biographer:

> . . . a moment of cold-war climax had come. It was necessary
> to call Russia's hand in the game of economic competition.
> Dulles firmly believed the Soviet Union was not in a position
> to deliver effectively on all her economic propaganda of-
> fers. . . .
>
> It was necessary to demonstrate to friendly nations, by
> act rather than by oral explanation, that U.S. tolerance of
> nations which felt it necessary to stay out of Western de-
> fensive alliances could not brook the kind of insult Nasser
> presented in his repeated and accumulated unfriendly ges-
> tures.[40]
>
> It was necessary to make the demonstration on a grand
> scale. . . . Nasser combined the right timing, the right geog-
> raphy, and the right order of magnitude for a truly major
> gambit in the cold war. . . .
>
> As a calculated risk the decision was on a grand scale,
> comparable in the sphere of diplomacy to the calculated
> risks of war taken in Korea and Formosa. . . .
>
> Dulles' bet was placed on his belief that it would expose
> the shallow character of Russia's foreign economic preten-
> sions. . . . He risked the prestige of the United States on
> those beliefs, knowing that it would bring reaction on a com-
> mensurate scale.[41]

But it was not, after all, the prestige of the United States that
was being gambled with—despite the semblance of a calculated risk—but that of two of her expendable "allies."

*   *   *   *   *

[In the course of a political scandal in Israel in the fall of 1960, veiled reference was made to "a disastrous security operation" in 1954, which was generally connected with the alleged espionage and sabotage group brought to trial in Egypt at that time. An editorial in *The Times* ("The Lavon Affair," November 3, 1960) asked whether this "security operation" had been "a clumsy attempt to exacerbate relations between the United States and Egypt by promoting what would look like sabotage acts against American institutions in Egypt." If the Israeli Army did attempt such an *agent-provocateur* operation, it bore much greater responsibility for the chain of events leading to the Egyptian-Soviet arms deal than has been implied in this chapter.]

CHAPTER 4

THE GREAT DIVORCE

The imperialist policy which the U.S.S.R. had already begun to follow in Eastern Europe before the end of World War II led to a close identification of U.S. and British interests and therefore to an alignment of policies for the defense of what could be salvaged in that continent. But it was much more difficult to achieve any such coordination of U.S. and British policies in the Middle East. During the past century, that region had been one in which British imperialism had taken an increasing hold, culminating in the imperialist "settlement" after World War I; and though the British hold was now being relaxed, the challenge of the new Soviet imperialism led the British policy-makers—including those who sported the fading red tie of the Labour Party—to protract this transitional period lest a power vacuum result, to the ultimate advantage of the U.S.S.R. The United States, a "rather reluctant debutante" in the field of world affairs,[1] exhibited an anti-colonialist attitude in its eagerness to see the remnants of British and French imperialism swept away,[2] though it still retained a firm hold on such products of "Yankee imperialism" as the Panama Canal; the makers of U.S. policy were confident that nationalist regimes, their independence newly acquired, could be stiffened by injections of arms, dollars, and advice into becoming staunch defenders of the "free world" against Communist subversion.

Already, in the period 1945-49, there had been a serious divergence of U.S. and British policy over Palestine. Ernest Bevin had been advised by his Foreign Office specialists that British interests in the Middle East could be secured only by conciliating the Arab states, at the price of resisting the determined and sometimes unprincipled Zionist drive toward statehood. President Truman, on the other hand, appeared to be almost uncritically committed to the Zionist thesis, disregarding largely the future of U.S. interests in the Arab world. Thus, the United Nations was treated in 1947-48 to the spectacle of the U.S. and the U.S.S.R. voting together in support of Israel, against the Arab states and Britain.

Again, in the Anglo-Iranian oil dispute of 1951-53, the nationalism of Dr. Musaddiq won substantial sympathy in the United States until he wore it out by his unrealistic intransigence; and as late as March, 1953, when Anthony Eden visited Washington as Foreign Secretary to renew personal contacts with the men of the new Republican Administration, he found the Americans "perpetually eager to do something." President Eisenhower seemed ready "to go to considerable lengths to keep Musaddiq in power, since he regarded him as the only hope for the West in Iran. . . . He would like to send to Iran a man in whom the Iranians had confidence. . . . He seemed obsessed by the fear of a communist Iran. Musaddiq has evidently again scared the Americans."[3] Fortunately, a more robust outlook eventually prevailed, and Musaddiq's overthrow by a military *coup* in Tehran allegedly took place not without the connivance of some U.S. representatives there.

But another, more complicated abscess of Anglo-American disagreement already existed on the Arabian peninsula and was coming to a head. There the basic historical fact was that the first period of Saudi-Wahhabi domination in central Arabia had collapsed in internal dissensions around 1869, and some eastern tribes and localities on whom it had forcibly levied taxes (*zakat*)[4] intermittently during the preceding century had then found other, less exacting suzerains like the sheikhs of Abu Dhabi on the Trucial Coast. However, after Abdul Aziz ibn Saud, the future "Great King," had succeeded from 1901 onward in gradually restoring his dynastic domain, his ambitious spirit envisaged reincorporating into his kingdom of Saudi Arabia (this name was assumed in 1932) all the territories that had ever paid homage to Wahhabi sectarianism and tribute to his Saudi ancestors. Furthermore, once oil had begun to flow in huge quantities from the subsoil of his barren realm, the thought that this El Dorado might extend under the eastern wastes of the Empty Quarter (*ar-Rub' al-Khali*) further whetted the Great King's appetite. Wahhabi history confirms one lesson to be drawn from the history of the English-speaking peoples—that there is nothing like falling away from an earlier puritanism to stimulate an insatiable craving for material goods.[5]

While the Great King had granted a monopoly on the oil concession in his realm to the Arabian-American Oil Company (Aramco), the eastern principalities of Muscat and Oman and of the Trucial Coast had been induced by their British "protecting power"[6] to grant similar monopolies in oil concessions to subsidiaries of the Iraq Petroleum Company (IPC), which was registered in London but had United States participation in its stock to the extent of 23.75 per cent. There was considerable local rivalry between these two companies; and after World War II, when the rival companies began sending prospecting parties into the hinterland of the Trucial Coast (regions whose frontiers had never been defined) and into the interior of Oman (where the writ of the Sultan in Muscat had not been effective among the tribes for many years[7]), the Saudi King advanced a claim in 1949 extending eastward some fifty miles beyond what his ministers had claimed in negotiations in 1935, taking in the whole of the Empty Quarter and the strategically situated oasis of Buraimi:

> . . . the only well-watered locality in northern Oman and, as such, the natural resort of all travelers crossing the great desert from the west. As the crossroads of the principal routes from the west and from the Gulf coast into Oman proper, Buraimi possesses a particular strategic value: whoever holds the oasis can dominate the Trucial Sheikhdoms to the north and the Sultanate of Oman to the east and, conversely, no invading force from the west, bent on the subjection of those principalities, could afford to bypass Buraimi and leave its lines of communication exposed.[8]

To fortify this claim, in 1952 the Arab Research Division of Aramco compiled, in Arabic and English, for restricted circulation a volume entitled *Oman and the Southern Shore of the Gulf,*[9] which not only rehearsed evidence purporting to substantiate the Saudi claim, but also defined inner Oman as a state independent of the Sultan in Muscat, although no such state had ever had international recognition and "relations between the . . . Sultan . . . and the inland tribes would appear to have been harmonious if somewhat distant" since the conclusion of an extremely ambiguous *modus vivendi* between them in 1920 (the so-called Treaty of Sib).[10] In August, 1952, protracted boundary negotiations between the Saudi Government and the British protecting power for the eastern principalities having reached a deadlock, a Saudi official named Turki ibn Ataishan arrived at Buraimi with some forty armed followers—there is little doubt that they moved

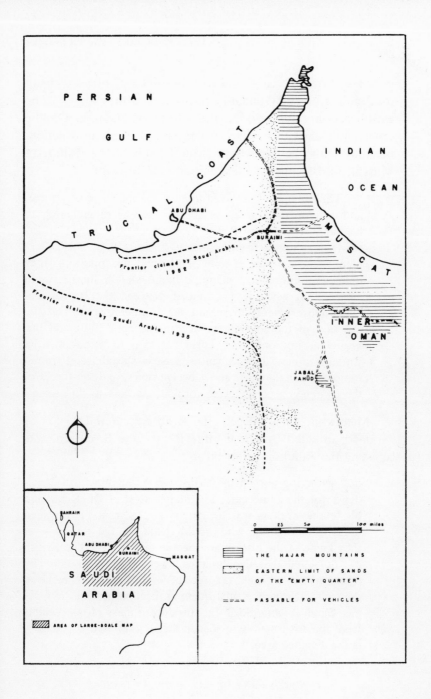

PERSIAN

GULF

INDIAN

OCEAN

TRUCIAL COAST

ABU DHABI

BURAIMI

MUSCAT

Frontier claimed by Saudi Arabia, 1952

Frontier claimed by Saudi Arabia, 1935

INNER
OMAN

JABAL
FAHŪD

0   25   50   100 miles

THE HAJAR MOUNTAINS

EASTERN LIMIT OF SANDS
OF THE "EMPTY QUARTER"

PASSABLE FOR VEHICLES

BAHRAIN

QATAR

ABU DHABI

BURAIMI

MASQAT

SAUDI

ARABIA

AREA OF LARGE-SCALE MAP

in Aramco transports[11]—and was welcomed by two sheikhs of the Naim tribe (of Wahhabi persuasion), with whose help he established his authority in the village of Hamasa. On the other hand, the other tribes of the oasis, having historic connections with the Sheikh of Abu Dhabi or the Sultan of Muscat, looked upon the expedition with disfavor.

> The Sultan . . . resolved to eject the interlopers by force, and tribesmen from all parts of Oman were gathering to his support when the British Government intervened to dissuade the Sultan from resorting to arms. . . . Instead, a blockade was imposed upon Turki and his followers: they managed, however, to maintain themselves in Buraimi until July, 1954, when it was agreed between the British and Saudi Governments to submit the frontier dispute and the question of the sovereignty of Buraimi to a "just and impartial arbitration." . . . Turki . . . was to withdraw from Buraimi immediately: a neutral zone was established around the oasis to a depth of about twelve miles, and the forces of the contending parties were forbidden access to this zone.[12]

Meanwhile, it is alleged, the Arab Research Division of Aramco, directed by Dr. George Rentz, a U.S. citizen, was assisting the Saudi Government in:

> . . . gathering (or, in the British view, manufacturing) evidence for the Saudi case. The major effort of Dr. Rentz and his fellow workers was to employ Arabs from the disputed areas as "relators," who would relate for the record what they knew of the history and people of the area. The British . . . claimed that the "relators" were obliged to sign (by thumbprint) a Saudi tax receipt each time they received their pay. During the subsequent arbitration hearings in Geneva, Saudi Arabia did in fact produce a mass of tax receipts from the tribesmen as evidence that it exercised sovereignty in the disputed area.[13]

The Saudi Governor of the oilfield province of al-Hasa continued to send instructions to the commander of the small
Saudi police detachment (allowed, under the Anglo-Saudi
agreement, to remain in Buraimi pending arbitration) to make
payments to the local sheikhs, although surreptitiously "for
the agreement does not allow this";[14] and the Saudis supplied
funds and arms (as did Nasser's regime in Egypt as well) to
Sheikh Ghalib ibn Ali, who in 1954 assumed the Imamate of
inner Oman on the death of the previous incumbent of that
office, and encouraged him to make that region independent
of the Sultan in Muscat.[15] Furthermore, the British were to
produce a brother of the Sheikh of Abu Dhabi who testified to
a Saudi attempt to promote a *coup d'état* in that sheikhdom
during 1954.[16]

The tribunal appointed to conduct an "impartial arbitra-
tion" of the Buraimi dispute consisted of a Saudi and a British
member (respectively, Sheikh Yusuf Yasin, the Saudi Deputy
Foreign Minister, and Sir Reader Bullard, formerly British
Minister to Saudi Arabia) and three neutral jurists drawn
from Belgium (which provided the president of the tribunal),
Cuba, and Pakistan. The Saudi case was in the hands of an
international panel of lawyers, led by the Egyptian Abd ur-
Rahman Azzam (formerly Secretary-General of the Arab
League) and including Professor Manley O. Hudson of Harvard Law School and his assistant, Richard Young.[17] The
opening of the tribunal at Geneva in September, 1955, was
delayed for a week because the Pakistani member, who was
making the Muslim pilgrimage to Mecca (in Saudi Arabia!),
had not yet arrived; the celebrated Arabian traveler H. St. J.
B. Philby, for many years a strong partisan of the Saudi
Government, later remarked that "during the initial discussions
of arrangements for the Buraimi arbitration, Yusuf Yasin . . .
tried to curry favor in advance with the neutral arbitrators by

suggesting fantastic sums for their services."[18] When it then became clear to Sir Reader Bullard that, in the course of the tribunal's hearings, Sheikh Yusuf Yasin had seen fit to brief the principal Saudi witness as to his evidence and conduct before the tribunal and was "representing that Government . . . rather than acting as an impartial arbitrator," Sir Reader announced his own resignation on September 16;[19] this was followed by the resignation of the Belgian president a week later and by the resignation of the Cuban member shortly afterward, thus bringing the work of the tribunal to an end.

An American magazine and a British weekly concurred that the resignation of these two neutral members stemmed from their disapproval of the Saudi methods,[20] and there was a British disposition to concede that Saudi conceptions of impartial arbitration differed widely from those prevailing in Europe;[21] but the Saudis elaborated a charge that Bullard's resignation had been a last-minute device to forestall a judgment unfavorable to the British case.[22] The British Government did not answer this charge; instead, it seems, they had been making preparations to meet the possibility of a fresh breach with the Saudis:

> The Trucial Oman Scouts, British-officered and financed, which had been disbanded in early 1954 as the result of a mutiny, were re-formed. To supplement this force, Sir Stephen Gibson, managing director of IPC, made an agreement with the Sultan of Muscat to finance an army to assure the security of Oman. It was clear that this agreement . . . was one that could hardly have been approved by a responsible private company without the backing of the British Government. . . . It was presumably for this reason (and to keep the U.S. Government in the dark) that the IPC management did not—until several months later— inform its two American partners, Standard of New Jersey and Socony Mobil.

When this force had been raised, equipped, and trained, Britain acted with alacrity.[23]

Sir Anthony Eden summarized before the House of Commons on October 26 the Saudi conduct, which he said had made a fair and impartial arbitration impossible. He went on to say:

> Her Majesty's Government have therefore felt obliged, in the exercise of their duty to protect the legitimate interests of the Ruler of Abu Dhabi and the Sultan of Muscat, to advise them that the attempt to reach a just compromise by means of arbitration has failed. The forces of these Rulers, supported by the Trucial Oman levies, have accordingly this morning taken steps to resume their previous control of the Buraimi Oasis, and areas to the west of it. My latest information is that the Saudi force has been evacuated from the Buraimi Oasis, its only casualties being two men slightly wounded.[24]

The Foreign Secretary further stated, on November 6, in answer to a parliamentary question:

> The Buraimi problem was discussed with the State Department in September and they were warned of our view that Saudi conduct had made a continuation of arbitration virtually impossible. Her Majesty's Government did not give the United States authorities advance information of the decision that the Rulers concerned should resume control of the area, lest such foreknowledge should prove embarrassing to them in their relations with Saudi Arabia.[25]

It has since been alleged, by the same American writer who described IPC as enjoying the "backing" of the British Government, that the State Department "lacked all along . . . the will to make a stand" in this Arabian dispute, and that in 1954 continuous Aramco "pressures" were "effective in driving the State Department back to the position of safe neutrality from which it had begun to emerge."[26] When Sir Anthony

Eden visited Washington in January, 1956, President Eisenhower warned him that he should:

> . . . take account of world opinion. People in general, he maintained, were very ignorant about Muscat and Buraimi, and tended to think that the whole Arabian peninsula belonged, or ought to belong, to King Saud. Naturally we contested this, which took no account of the continuous expansion of Saudi claims ever since 1935. It also ignored the Yemen and Muscat, the independent sheikhdoms in the Persian Gulf, and ourselves in Aden. It certainly showed the dangers of oversimplification.

Later on, during the Suez crisis, Eden learned that:

> . . . the United States Government had regarded our action . . . in furthering the reoccupation of Buraimi . . . as an act of aggression. This opinion was expressed to . . . Australia and the Netherlands, but not to us. . . . When our Dutch friends asked Mr. Dulles who had ever suggested that there was any aggression by the United Kingdom at Buraimi, Mr. Dulles replied, "Public opinion in Saudi Arabia." He left himself open to the Dutch rejoinder that there was no such thing.[27]

Thus, a dispute between medieval princes in an obscure tract of a vast (but possibly oil-rich) desert was putting a new and serious strain on relations between the United States and the United Kingdom. A special correspondent in Washington commented on a tendency there to "smile a little superciliously at the handfuls of captured documents, revealing Saudi complicity in bribery, which the British had acquired at Buraimi and communicated to the State Department."[28] In Britain, in a debate on Middle Eastern policy immediately after the expulsion of Glubb Pasha from Jordan (which was partially the result of agitation subsidized by the Saudi Government

with money accruing from Aramco's advance payments of
royalties), members of all parties expressed irritation at the
"absurd" and "ludicrous" competition between the oil companies.[29] Two days later, Archbishop Makarios of Cyprus and
three of his principal associates were deported by the British
for their complicity in the campaign of violence abortively
seeking the union of Cyprus with Greece; and there were
British complaints when the U.S. Ambassador to Greece conveyed to that government his personal sympathy.[30] From the
American side came reports that "the United States is drawing
away from support of colonial powers";[31] "the United States
allows itself to become vulnerable to accusations of aiding and
abetting colonialism which is the No. 1 international enemy in
the Arab world";[32] "the U.S. Government was irritated by the
British Government's recent attempts to roar like a nineteenth-
century lion."[33]

Meanwhile, Eden had been in Washington on a visit beginning January 30, 1956, and had tried (1) to "put teeth into
the Tripartite Declaration of 1950," in which the U.S., British,
and French Governments had agreed to maintain the *status
quo* between the Arab states and Israel that was now threatened by the Egyptian-Soviet arms deal and Abdel Nasser's
exploitation of the *fedayeen;* (2) to regulate the situation in
eastern Arabia; and (3) to persuade the U.S. Government to
take a more positive attitude toward the Baghdad Pact, which
was being constantly assailed by Egyptian, Saudi, and Syrian
subversion and propaganda:

> In recent years the United States has sometimes failed
> to put its weight behind its friends, in the hope of being
> popular with their foes. The practical consequences of this
> uncertain diplomacy are illustrated by United States treat-
> ment of the Baghdad Pact. . . .
> A strong power, rich in resources, once it determines

its goal, has a fair chance to reach it, if it holds to its purpose. A devious course is disastrous. It is a borrower and lender in diplomacy and loses both itself and friend.[34]

Eden admits that he "probably . . . overvalued the political results" of these conversations in Washington; and by the beginning of April, it was evident that the U.S. Government, increasingly absorbed in the Presidential election campaign, had tacitly rejected new and apparently urgent representations from Eden concerning the worsening Middle East situation.[35] On April 7, Joseph C. Harsch commented in *The Christian Science Monitor*:

> The old British position is being washed away at a rate which has alarmed and shaken the government in London. But . . . John Foster Dulles and President Eisenhower this week refused to share London's alarm about the matter. They would not agree that the position was critical. . . .
>
> It was a profoundly novel fact this week that on the Middle Eastern issue *Washington was operating more closely with Moscow than with London*. . . . It was a week of crisis in the Anglo-American alliance.[36]

Thus, already in April, 1956, the dragon's teeth of mutual incomprehension had been sown, from which the armed men were to spring in the monstrous birth of the Suez crisis six months later.

Nor did the relationship improve in the intervening months, while the Secretary-General of the United Nations, at the instance of the United States, vainly tried to allay the tension between Egypt and Israel. Joseph Alsop, of the *New York Herald Tribune,* after a lengthy journey of inquiry in the Middle East, reported on June 27 (four weeks before Abdel Nasser's confiscation of the Suez Canal) that he found:

> . . . a pernicious tendency, not least in the State Department, to take Britain for granted. If the Middle Eastern problem

has any meaning at all, it very clearly means that Britain cannot prudently be taken for granted any longer . . . because the real foundations of the British structure are still colonial and imperial; and these foundations are now in grave danger. . . .

The British policy-makers understand the danger of British bankruptcy, which means the end of Britain's career as a major power. As Sir Anthony Eden has said, they are convinced that the loss of Cyprus will be only the preliminary to the loss of the Middle Eastern oil sources. So the British have reacted violently, too violently in this reporter's opinion. But so should we react very violently, if we felt hostile hands groping for our jugular.

In these circumstances, it is amazing and pretty terrifying to come home, and to discover that the State Department's chief parlor game seems to be smug carping at the British policy in such places as Cyprus and Buraimi.

What does it matter if Britain's struggles to defend her own jugular have become pretty convulsive, compared to the hard fact that this same Britain also happens to be the jugular of the United States?

But, as Eden had already written in 1954 in connection with the crisis in French Indochina:

Americans may think the time past when they need consider the feelings or difficulties of their allies. It is the conviction that this tendency becomes more pronounced every week that is creating mounting difficulties for anyone in this country who wants to maintain close Anglo-American relations.[37]

It was herein that the somber drama of the Suez crisis lay. By confiscating the Canal in a *crise de prestige* only six weeks after his government had confirmed the Canal Company's concession,[38] Gamal Abdel Nasser showed himself to be a lesser specimen of the Hitler breed[39]—a political opportunist

who comes within an ace of genius as a tactician, but a moral
featherweight. And just as, in the Anglo-French drama of the
Second Syrian War of 1839-40, the personality of Mohammed
Ali Pasha of Egypt shrank to the dimensions of a minor character,[40] so Abdel Nasser receded to the status of a mere co-
respondent in the Anglo-American "great divorce" over Suez.

The speed with which Egyptian officers forcibly took over
the operations of the Suez Canal Company on July 26, 1956,
indicated that the seizure was no improvisation, but had been
carefully planned. On the other hand, there is no evidence that
the seizure would have occurred *at that time,* had it not been
triggered by Dulles' peremptory withdrawal of the High Dam
offer. Though Dulles apparently tried to evade this obvious
inference,[41] he tacitly admitted it when he hurried to London
and spoke in the following manner to the British Government
on August 1:

> A way had to be found to make Nasser disgorge what
> he was attempting to swallow. . . . We must make a genuine
> effort to bring world opinion to favor the international
> operation of the Canal. . . . It should be possible to create
> a world opinion so adverse to Nasser that he would be
> isolated. Then if a military operation had to be undertaken
> it would be more apt to succeed and have less grave reper-
> cussions than if it had been undertaken precipitately.

Eden says that he told Dulles during these first consultations:

> . . . that the United States Naval Attaché had been asking
> for information about our military preparations. I said that
> we were quite ready to give this, but that we wanted first
> to make sure that the United States Government really
> wished to have it. Mr. Dulles replied that the United States
> Government perfectly well understood the purpose of our
> preparations and *he thought that they had had a good effect.*
> It was preferable that the United States Government should
> not seek detailed information.

From Washington, on the other hand, the British Ambassador:

> . . . had already reported . . . that he had found the State
> Department cool and hesitant about taking urgent action.
> The Department gave the impression of wishing to stand
> aloof from the dispute with Egypt. Its officials were much
> concerned about the effects of any possible action on Ameri-
> can public opinion.[42]

When the Suez crisis was debated for the first time in the
British House of Commons on August 2, there was virtual
unanimity. Hugh Gaitskell, the leader of the Opposition, was
officially reported as saying:

> If Colonel Nasser's prestige is put up sufficiently and
> ours is put down sufficiently, the effects of that . . . will be
> that our friends desert us because they think we are lost,
> and go over to Egypt.
>
> I have no doubt myself that the reason why Colonel
> Nasser acted in the way he did, aggressively, brusquely, sud-
> denly, was precisely because he wanted to raise his prestige
> in the rest of the Middle East. . . . He wanted to assert his
> strength. He wanted to make a big impression. . . . It is all
> very familiar. It is exactly the same that we encountered
> from Mussolini and Hitler in the years before the war.[43]

Beginning early in August, however:

> Left-wing and doubtful-minded journals saw in the pos-
> sible use of force a handy stick with which to beat the
> [British] Government, [and] . . . did not hesitate to employ
> it. . . .
>
> On August 13th the Opposition Shadow Cabinet issued a
> statement. The retreat then began amid a clatter of excuses.
> The most contradictory of these maintained that forcible
> action was certainly justified if it had the sanction of the
> United Nations. From the first the Soviet Government made
> it plain that it would give diplomatic support to the Egyp-
> tians. This meant that Moscow would run no risks, but would

take every political pot-shot from behind cover. The use of
the veto in the Security Council was the easiest of these. . . .

It is pardonable not to see the danger. It is excusable to
see it and declare it and do nothing effective about it on
moral grounds. It is unpardonable to see it and make a pretense of meeting it by methods one knows in one's heart to
be totally ineffective. . . .

The instability of opinion [in Britain] was very much less
than it was pictured to be. But there can be no question
that what was believed to be the deep division in the country
created difficulties for our diplomacy from the start. Doubt
about British national unity had its repercussions in the
United States. It was constantly quoted . . . by American
negotiators and helped to weaken American resolution.[44]

It is probably no exaggeration to say that after the internal
dissensions in the British Labour Party which followed its fall
from power in 1950-51, the party sought and found a cheap
anodyne in exploiting their Tory rivals' difficulties in the area
of imperial policy. The worsening Cyprus situation from 1954
onward gave them an opportunity which they grasped with
avidity. The Baghdad Pact, Jordan, Suez, Oman, the Anglo-
American Middle East intervention in July, 1958, complica-
tions in Central and East Africa followed—*facilis descensus
Averno*—until (at the time of writing) the latest point in this
progressive irresponsibility (following Labour's third successive rejection by the electorate in 1959) was their combination
of half-informed emotionalism and cynical party tactics in
setting off the inflammable human material in the Union of
South Africa.[45]

Until August 23, 1956, when eighteen of the twenty-two
governments represented at the London Conference[46] sub-
scribed to the principle of international control for the Canal
while accepting the accomplished fact of its "nationalization,"

the Anglo-American front remained apparently firm. But at
this stage, says Eden:

> The United Kingdom Government had to determine what
> action to take if Nasser turned down the proposals of the
> eighteen powers. . . . We wished to refer the issue to the
> Security Council, if Nasser declared his unwillingness to ne-
> gotiate. We also desired as many powers as possible to exert
> financial and economic pressure upon Egypt. The United
> States discouraged us in both these initiatives.
>
> While Mr. Dulles was still in London we had again urged
> upon him the importance of denying the Canal dues to
> Nasser. . . . The United States Government never agreed to
> effective action. . . .
>
> The United States Government were not helpful about
> other forms of financial restraint. . . . Dulles . . . felt that he
> had first to pave the way with the American public for any
> further steps. In the event, no paving was ever done. On his
> return to Washington, Dulles spoke to our Ambassador of
> keeping a number of alternatives in view. In principle, he was
> in favor of economic measures, but all he could promise was
> that the United States Government should prepare to take
> them. In fact, they never took them. . . .
>
> The course of the Suez Canal crisis was decided by the
> American attitude to it. If the United States Government had
> approached this issue in the spirit of an ally, they would have
> done everything in their power, short of the use of force, to
> support the nations whose economic security depended upon
> the freedom of passage through the Suez Canal. They would
> have closely planned their policies with their allies and held
> stoutly to the decisions arrived at. They would have insisted
> on restoring international authority in order to insulate the
> canal from the politics of any one country. It is now clear
> that this was never the attitude of the United States Govern-
> ment. Rather did they try to gain time, coast along over
> difficulties as they arose and improvise policies, each follow-

ing on the failure of its immediate predecessor. None of these was geared to the long-term purpose of serving a joint cause.[47]

Instead, states the latest American appraisal of Dulles' policy:[48]

> Dulles embarked on what proved to be a fatally ineffective course. He played Eden along from week to week, for more than a month. . . . He tried to gain time until Eden's resolve to attack Egypt[49] might weaken. He let Eden gain the impression that Washington would not oppose an Anglo-French invasion if all attempts at negotiation failed. When closeted with Eden, he gave the impression of being at one with him in his aversion to Nasser. In public, however, he infuriated Eden by pointedly disassociating the United States from British colonialism.
>
> One of his main time-gaining devices was a legalistically skillful proposal for a multi-national Suez Canal Users' Association.[50]

While Dulles was working on this proposal during a short holiday in Ontario, Eden received on September 3 a "disquieting message" from President Eisenhower, described by Eden as follows:

> Hitherto he and his officials had always given us to understand that the United States would not take exception to the use of force, if all peaceful means of settlement had been exhausted. The fact that we had taken military precautions had, furthermore, been approved from time to time. Now the President told me that American public opinion flatly rejected force. He admitted that the procedures of negotiation on which we were then engaged would probably not give Nasser the setback he deserved. But he advised that we should sharply separate the question of the Canal from our

general policy towards the Egyptian dictatorship and the menace under which Africa and the Middle East lay. The latter he considered a long-term problem.[51]

In fact, as an American military historian has remarked in his review of Eden's *Memoirs,* what the United States Government wanted at this time was a "settlement" that would paste everything up in acceptable fashion and would enable Eisenhower to win the 1956 election as an "apostle of peace."[52]

Eden, on the other hand, emphasized in his reply to the President the conviction of his government and of the French that the seizure of the Suez Canal was:

". . . the opening gambit in a planned campaign designed by Nasser to expel all Western influence and interests from Arab countries. He believes that . . . if he can successfully defy eighteen nations, his prestige in Arabia will be so great that he will be able to mount revolutions of young officers in Saudi Arabia, Jordan, Syria, and Iraq. (We know that he is already preparing a revolution in Iraq.) . . . These new Governments . . . will have to place their united oil resources under the control of a united Arabia led by Egypt and under Russian influence. When that moment comes Nasser can deny oil to Western Europe and we here shall all be at his mercy. . . .

"We are convinced that if Nasser is allowed to defy the eighteen nations it will be a matter of months before revolution breaks out in the oil-bearing countries and the West is wholly deprived of Middle Eastern oil. In this belief we are fortified by the advice of friendly leaders in the Middle East.

"The Iraqis are the most insistent in their warnings; both Nuri and the Crown Prince have spoken to us several times of the consequences of Nasser succeeding in his grab. They would be swept away."

I then gave the President an account of three other warnings which we had received, each from a different Middle Eastern country: as the authors of these warnings are still alive, I do not propose to make their names public. . . .

"You may feel [Eden continued] that even if we are right it would be better to wait until Nasser has unmistakably unveiled his intentions. But this was the argument which prevailed in 1936 [Hitler's remilitarization of the Rhineland] and which we both rejected in 1948 [Stalin's Berlin blockade]. Admittedly there are risks in the use of force against Egypt now. It is, however, clear that military intervention designed to reverse Nasser's revolutions in the whole continent would be a much more costly and difficult undertaking. I am very troubled, as it is, that if we do not reach a conclusion either way about the Canal very soon one or other of these eastern lands may be toppled at any moment by Nasser's revolutionary movements. . . .

"I can assure you that we are conscious of the burdens and perils attending military intervention. But if our assessment is correct, and if the only alternative is to allow Nasser's plans quietly to develop until this country and all Western Europe are held to ransom by Egypt acting at Russia's behest it seems to us that our duty is plain. We have many times led Europe in the fight for freedom. It would be an ignoble end to our long history if we accepted to perish by degrees."[53]

On September 7, Dulles informed the British Ambassador that "he would find it very difficult to go along with" the Anglo-French resolution submitted to the Security Council "in its present form," and urged the two governments:

. . . for the time being, merely to inform the Security Council of the situation by letter and ask for no action. . . . Even then, the United States Government declined to add their signature to our letter. We were told that they did not wish to create an identity of interest, which might prove embarrassing to the French and ourselves. . . .

[The Foreign Secretary] urged the absolute necessity for effective action. Delay would be disastrous for a number of reasons. Every day Nasser was strengthening his hold on the Canal. The Western powers would lose face unless they could react clearly and speedily to his rejection of the eighteen-power proposals, which now seemed certain. Meanwhile the friendly Arab states were in great and ever-increasing peril.

Her Majesty's Government . . . did not believe that the Canal issue could be separated from the general Egyptian menace to the friendly governments of the Muslim world.[54]

It was at this stage that Dulles produced his "latest formulation" of thoughts on a Suez Canal Users' Association:

Putting Mr. Dulles' plan into effect was to be accompanied, he told us, by two further prongs of attack. One prong was provided by the financial measures which the French and ourselves had already taken, but in respect of which the United States continued to lag behind.[55] The other prong was the rerouting of oil traffic . . . to decrease our dependence upon the Canal.

In spite of certain "unwelcome implications" in the plan, which Eden describes, he decided to take it up. On September 12, he informed the House of Commons of the formation of the Canal Users' Association and employed the formula agreed upon with the U.S. Government in issuing the warning that if Egypt interfered with the working of the scheme, the governments concerned would "be free to take such further steps as seem to be required either through the United Nations, or by other means for the assertion of their rights."[56] Dulles openly dissented, however, and told a press conference on the following day:

We do not intend to shoot our way through. It may be we have the right to do it, but we don't intend to do it as far

as the United States is concerned. . . . Each nation has to
decide for itself what action it will have to take to defend
and, if possible, realize its rights which it believes it has as a
matter of treaty.[57]

Eden made the following comments:

It would be hard to imagine a statement more likely to
cause the maximum Allied disunity and disarray. The Americans having themselves volunteered that the new arrangements would be less acceptable to the Egyptians than the
eighteen-power proposals, Mr. Dulles proceeded to make
. . . an advertisement to Nasser that he could reject the
project with impunity. . . . Whatever happened, the Egyptians had nothing to fear. . . . Here was the spokesman of the
United States saying that each nation must decide for itself
and expressing himself as unable to recall what the spokesman of a principal ally had said.[58] *Such cynicism towards
allies destroys true partnership. It leaves only the choice of
parting, or a master and vassal relationship in foreign
policy.*

In the House I had, in fact . . . used the formula agreed
with the United States Government. . . . This left the course
of future action deliberately vague so as to strengthen pressure on behalf of the Users' Club. The whole purpose of the
Users' Club had been, by a display of unity in association
with the United States, to avoid having recourse to force.
American torpedoing of their own plan on the first day of
launching it, left no alternative but to use force or acquiesce
in Nasser's triumph.[59]

A second conference in London of fifteen "Canal users"
(meeting at a time when pilots from the U.S.S.R., Yugoslavia,
and the United States were being recruited by the Egyptian
Government) concluded its work on September 21 with a
declaration which was, in Eden's view:

. . . undoubtedly marked by some ambiguity and it had a cool, though not unfavorable, public reception. . . . It became clear to us only gradually that the American conception of the association was now evolving so fast that it would end as an agency for collecting dues for Nasser. . . .

Our information from the Middle East at this time confirmed the gloomy views we had been forming in London. . . . Opinion in Cairo . . . had been encouraged to think that Nasser had succeeded. . . .

The United States Government were still reluctant to approach the United Nations and we tried to meet them on this for a while longer. But the closing stage of the London Conference brought increasing pressure upon us to go to the Security Council.[60]

On October 1, after receiving a long pro-Egyptian letter from Marshal Bulganin (still the titular head of the Soviet Government, as Nagib had been in Egypt during 1952-54), Eden telegraphed to Eisenhower:

There is no doubt in our minds that Nasser, whether he likes it or not, is now effectively in Russian hands, just as Mussolini was in Hitler's. It would be as ineffective to show weakness to Nasser now in order to placate him as it was to show weakness to Mussolini. . . .

No doubt your people will have told you of the accumulating evidence of Egyptian plots in Libya, Saudi Arabia and Iraq. At any moment any of these may be touched off unless we can prove to the Middle East that Nasser is losing. That is why we are so concerned to do everything we can to make the Users' Club an effective instrument.[61]

While Eden's analogy between Abdel Nasser and Mussolini was no doubt open to debate, the gloss which Dulles put on the situation in a press conference the next day evoked in him "exasperation and dismay":

There is talk [said Dulles] about the "teeth" being pulled
out of [the Users' Club]. There were never "teeth" in it, if
that means the use of force. . . .

There has been some difference in our approach to this
problem of the Suez Canal. This is not an area where we are
bound together by treaty . . . such as the North Atlantic
Treaty area. . . . There . . . I hope and believe [we] always
will stand absolutely together.

There are also other problems where our approach is not
always identical. For example, there is in Asia and Africa
the so-called problem of colonialism. Now there the United
States plays a somewhat independent role. You have this very
great problem of the shift from colonialism to independence which is in process. . . . I suspect that the United States
will find that its role . . . will be to try to aid that process,
without identifying itself 100 per cent either with the colonial
powers or with the powers which are primarily and uniquely
concerned with the problems of getting their independence
as rapidly as possible.[62]

Eden comments:

If the United States had to defend their treaty rights in
the Panama Canal, they would not regard such action as
colonialism, neither would I. Yet their rights in Panama are
those of one nation, not of many nations, as at Suez.[63] . . .

From the outset, however, there had been in all countries
those who were not prepared to see this dispute for what it
was, the denial of an international engagement, recently re-
affirmed by the Egyptian Government, and the seizure by
force of international property. They preferred to look upon
it as the expression of a nationalist mood in a country
recently emancipated, for which, therefore, benevolent allow-
ances must be made. . . .

The newspapers in New York now reported that the
American delegation [to the United Nations] were openly

talking of "rifts" between themselves and their French and British colleagues. . . . The Foreign Secretary [Selwyn Lloyd] took this up direct with the Secretary of State.[64]

Mr. Dulles . . . declared that he was with Britain on every point, except the use of force. *Even force he did not rule out as an ultimate resort,* and he once more recognized our right to maintain the threat of using it. Nevertheless, he felt that to employ force in the immediate future would be a mistake, since in his view Nasser's position was deteriorating. There seemed no grounds for this last estimate.[65]

In British and French eyes, the vital part of the resolution placed before the Security Council was the declaration "that the Users' Association should receive the dues payable by the ships of its members, and that the association and the Egyptian nationalized authority should cooperate to ensure the satisfactory management of the Canal." This section obtained nine affirmative votes out of eleven, but was vetoed by the U.S.S.R. Eden comments:

We were left with six principles, and principles are aimless unless translated into action. . . . They just flapped in the air. Nor had a time limit been set to the interchanges expected of the French, British and Egyptian Governments. The way was open to endless procrastination by Egypt. Worse, it also lay open to her to renew her aggressive designs in other fields. . . .

Though the Americans had been the first advocates of these proposals [made by the eighteen powers in August], the Administration showed no concern at their defeat by the Communist veto. Beaming through rose-coloured spectacles, they acclaimed the six principles in their place. . . . I was not surprised when messages from our friends in the Middle East showed dismay at Nasser's swelling success.

It was clear enough to me where we were. . . . It was of no use to fool ourselves. . . . We had been strung along over many months of negotiation from pretext to pretext, from device to device, and from contrivance to contrivance. . . .

The Soviets had had their way and no amount of soothing optimism could conceal the truth.

Yet the notion gained currency that the Security Council had prepared the terms for a peaceful and just settlement of the dispute. . . .

Perhaps the most disturbing feature of all these discussions was the utter indifference shown by the United Nations to the international aspects of the crisis. . . . From the start to the end of the business, not one single syllable of censure or regret was uttered . . . by the Security Council or by the General Assembly, at, the seizure of a great international waterway by force. It is inevitable that there will be a reckoning for this moral backsliding.[66]

The reader will appreciate the irony of Eden's appeal to morality, in view of the "contempt of truth" and "saber-rattling jingoism" which was the imputation that the leader of Her Majesty's Opposition placed upon his policy.[67] A moralist less affected by party interest has remarked more justly that "Eden's moral dilemma has a lasting significance. In trying to preserve the political conditions of international life he became doctrinaire; in trying to enforce the moral conditions of international life he allowed himself to become unscrupulous . . . high-mindedness and self-righteousness, blindness and clearsightedness, misjudgment and courage."[68]

Eden continues his narrative:

There had been a suggestion at the United Nations for a meeting between representatives of [the] French and Egyptian Governments and ourselves at Geneva. . . .

An agreement of sorts about the Canal . . . might have been dressed up to look fairly reasonable, even though I knew that it did not mean much. . . . I could not return from Geneva with a piece of paper and commend it to the

House of Commons, when I knew that it had no real value. This would have reassured the world about a dictator whose intentions were, I was sure, predatory. Those who did not wish to face unpleasant realities would have been encouraged. . . . I had been through so much of this before. . . .

The Security Council was no sooner over than the Egyptians began to plead excuses against even the principles which they had accepted. The Government decided meanwhile to align their views with the French Government who were their partners in these talks. It was all the more necessary to do so, because the Middle Eastern scene began to look threatening again; the immediate consequence of weakness.[69]

When Eden and Selwyn Lloyd flew to Paris on October 16 to confer with the French Prime Minister and Foreign Minister (Guy Mollet and Pineau), one of the subjects they discussed was their "disappointment" at Dulles' message of the day before concerning the Users' Association proposals:

The general American complaint was that we were concerned with [their] punitive character . . . whereas the United States Government regarded them as a means of cooperating with Egypt. This was not how they had been originally described to us. . . . We saw the Users' Club being increasingly organized as an agency to forward dues to Egypt. There was a danger of absurdity in this. At that time 60 per cent of the Canal dues were being denied to Nasser by the ships of Britain, France and others who had followed our lead. From what Mr. Dulles had told the Foreign Secretary, it appeared that nine-tenths of this 60 per cent was to be handed over to Egypt. . . . The only gain to the users would be that they would retain one-tenth of the 3 per cent of Canal dues paid by ships flying the American flag. Nasser would have every reason to be grateful to the Users' Club. . . .

He was now to be paid infinitely more than anything he had been offered before.

Exasperated by this appeasement of the Egyptian dictator by the United States at the expense of her allies, the British and French ministers discussed the dangers of the general situation in the Levant:

> The line-up between Jordan, Egypt and Syria was becoming ever closer. There were reports of the establishment of a joint command under Egyptian direction, which in fact soon came into existence [October 23]. Cairo radio blared with increasing vehemence against Israel, menacing her with destruction. Unless Israel was prepared just to sit and wait until it suited her enemies to strangle and finally destroy her, it was clear that before long she would have to take some counter-action, at least to put an end to the *fedayeen* raids.[70] If directed against Jordan, from which some of the *fedayeen* raids were said to be mounted under Egyptian leadership,[71] then the position for us would be terrible indeed. We had a treaty obligation to defend Jordan. . . .
>
> Therefore, at this meeting in Paris, we asked the French Ministers to do everything they could to make clear to Israel that an attack on Jordan would have to be resisted by us. This they undertook to do. . . . If Israel were to break out against Egypt and not against Jordan, this dilemma would not arise. For this reason, *if there were to be a breakout it was better from our point of view that it should be against Egypt.* On the other hand, if the break-out were against Egypt, then there would be other worries, for example the safety of the Canal. . . .[72]

It was after this fateful meeting in Paris, where the groundwork for the notorious "collusion" with Israel was evidently laid[73] (Eden is discreetly silent on this point), that the British Foreign Office imposed what Dulles afterward described as a "blackout" on its communications with Washington: "No longer was there daily consultation across the Atlantic on plans for peaceful action."[74] Dulles and President Eisenhower be-

came increasingly chagrined. But had they legitimate cause
for remonstrance, when it was they who had failed to make
any response to Eden's urgent warnings six months earlier,
and when as late as June the State Department's "chief parlor
game" had seemed to a responsible American commentator to
be "smug carping at the British policy"? In Eden's words,
"such cynicism towards allies [left] . . . only the choice of
parting, or a master and vassal relationship."[75] The breakdown
in communication and its consequences were both deplorable;
but to pretend that Washington bore none of the responsibility
for it exemplified the type of pharisaism which seemed natural
to that Administration.[76]

As Eden and his colleagues now surveyed the scene, the
kind of "drifting" which seemed to be the U.S. Government's
substitute for a policy

> . . . spelt certain disaster for the West's authority and meant
> an Arab-Israel war, fought under conditions most perilous
> for the peace of the whole area. Intervention by the Western
> powers, with all its risks, was clearly to be preferred. Nasser
> was well aware of this, and guarded all the more carefully
> against a direct provocation. He was not ready for that, yet.
> . . . Unchecked over Suez, he set to work upon the next
> projects. . . . These were to increase his supply of armaments
> from Communist sources, to undermine those Arab leaders
> who were in his way, and to tighten the noose around Israel,
> whose destruction in his own time was his declared objective.
>
> In existing circumstances it was idle to hope for effec-
> tive action by the United States or the United Nations. Left
> to itself the United Nations would never move, as its melan-
> choly record in Middle Eastern events clearly showed. If
> led or goaded by others, it might do so.[77]

Meanwhile, as the Israeli Ambassador to the United States
had prepared in early October to make a brief visit to Israel,

President Eisenhower sent him (through Dulles) an admonitory message, which the President afterward recalled as follows:

> I hoped that he would not allow any misinterpretation of sentiment in [the U.S.] to sway him, and particularly because of possible Jewish sympathy for . . . what seemed to be an intention of building up [sic] around the mobilization of Israel at that time—I hoped he would not allow this to sway his judgment as to what this Administration would do in doing [sic] its very best to prevent any outbreak of hostilities and . . . the settlement of international issues by force.
>
> And I told him that if he thought that this would have any . . . iota of influence on the [U.S. Presidential] election or that that would have any influence on me, he should disabuse his mind of it.[78]

It is interesting to speculate what effect this admonition (if, indeed, the President's memory did not play him false as to its contents as well as the channel of its communication)[79] had upon the formidable Ben-Gurion; but on October 25:

> . . . reports reached the State Department from Israel that the country apparently was beginning a military mobilization. The following day another cable reported these suspicious elements: the French and British seemed to know more about what was going on than did the Americans, but were evasive in talking.[80]

Eden comments:

> I thought then, and I think now, that the Israelis had justification for their action. . . . The marked victim of the garrotter is not to be condemned if he strikes out before the noose is round his throat.
>
> If we were not prepared to condemn Israel, we could

not stand aside and watch events. . . . The chief peril to us lay not in the [Israeli-Egyptian] conflict but in its extension by the intervention of other Arab states. The best way to halt them was by intervening ourselves . . . to occupy key positions at Port Said, Ismailia, and Suez. Our purpose was to safeguard free passage through the Canal, if it were threatened with becoming a zone of warfare, and to arrest the spread of fighting in the Middle East.

To realize this we would put into operation the plan for occupation of the Suez Canal Zone, prepared by the joint Anglo-French military staff which had been studying the problem since the end of July. . . .

Of course there were dangers in this policy. But there were dangers in any policy . . . not least in that of complete inaction. Political decisions, especially when they concern the Middle East, usually involve a choice of evils.[81] I am convinced that we chose the lesser evil.

Eden's telegram to Eisenhower on October 30, informing him of the Anglo-French intention to intervene following the Israeli advance into Egyptian territory the previous evening and inviting his general support, crossed a message from the President in which he:

. . . considered it of the greatest importance that the United Kingdom and the United States should quickly and clearly lay out their present views before each other, so that they might not in any real crisis be powerless to act in concert because of misunderstanding. That [says Eden drily] had been my purpose also at the January meeting in Washington, and all through this drawn-out business. . . .

The American Administration was urgently proposing to have Israel branded as an aggressor by the Security Council. It was unmoved by the history of the dispute or Egypt's aggressive attitude and declared intentions against Israel.[82]
. . . To denounce and neither to offer nor to accept any con-

structive suggestions was the core of American policy. . . .
The effect of the American proposal would have been to
condemn Anglo-French initiative, while substituting nothing
for it. . . .

The American representative pressed his resolution to a
vote with all speed and included in it phrases explicitly
directed against Anglo-French action. His only reply to the
arguments of the British representative, in public and in
private, was to ask the Council to take the vote at once. As
a result, Britain used her veto for the first time in her membership of the United Nations. . . .

*The Russians then moved a resolution substantially the
same as the American draft, but without its most offensive
paragraph* directed at the French and ourselves.[83]

After this veto in the Security Council, the issue was then
taken (by the deciding vote of the United States) to a special
session of the eighty-member General Assembly under the
makeshift "uniting for peace" procedure. There, on November 2:

. . . it was not Soviet Russia, or any Arab state, but the
Government of the United States which took the lead . . .
against Israel, France, and Britain. . . . There was no suggestion of going to the root of the matter. . . . There was no
attempt to snatch opportunity out of trouble, which is the
stamp of statesmanship. . . . Mr. Dulles recognized that a
resolution which merely sought to restore the *status quo*
before the Israeli attack was neither adequate nor compre-
hensive. He hoped that the United Nations would strive to
bring about a betterment of the conditions that had led to
. . . "this tragedy." He did not suggest how this could be
done.

The Canadian Minister for External Affairs . . . explained
why he could not vote for the United States resolution. . . .
He developed the idea, which [Eden] had advocated in the
House of Commons the day before, of a United Nations

police force . . . which would keep the peace on the frontiers
of Israel. . . .

Had the United States been willing to play a part as
balanced as Canada's, the course of history must have been
different, but this was not to be. The Assembly was in a
mood to punish. The hunt was up after Israel and the
"colonial" powers. Mr. Nixon, Vice President of the United
States, declared . . . "For the first time in history we have
shown independence of Anglo-French policies towards Asia
and Africa which seemed to us to reflect the colonial tradition. This declaration of independence has had an electrify-
ing effect throughout the world."[84]

"It is impossible," comments a reviewer, "not to detect the
note of relief, the fervour of genuine conviction" in this statement, and it was "the worst of Eden's miscalculations not to
have expected this reaction";[85] but if Eden erred, as many
Americans and British believed, in identifying Abdel Nasser
with Hitler and Mussolini, what shall we say of the U.S. Vice
President's facile equating of 1956 with 1776?

Meanwhile, the Russians had undertaken their repression
of the Hungarian revolt, about which Eden says:

Five days [after October 28] passed without any further
Council meeting upon Hungary, despite repeated attempts by
ourselves and others to bring one about. The United States
representative . . . voiced his suspicion that we were urging
the Hungarian situation to divert attention from Suez. The
United States Government appeared in no hurry to move.
Their attitude provided a damaging contrast to the alacrity
they were showing in arraigning the French and ourselves.[86]

As the editor chosen to write the annual summary for the
Council on Foreign Relations later admitted:

American policy thus turned out to be somewhat one-
sided in its effects. It helped to deprive France and England

of any advantages that might have been gained by their rash adventure; but it failed to penalize the U.S.S.R. in any equivalent way for what most people considered its wholly indefensible conduct in Hungary.[87]

At this point, Eden provides an interesting comment upon the state of public opinion in Britain, which was no more accurately represented by such organs of the "liberal intelligentsia" as *The Manchester Guardian, The Observer,* and the *New Statesman* than *The New Republic* and *The Nation* accurately reflect public opinion in the United States.[88] Eden says that the pressure of events gave him little time to study public opinion in detail, but he could obtain a "fair indication" from the contents of his mailbag:

> Letters were . . . at the outset something like eight to one against. With the passage of time, this majority weakened and finally disappeared until, in the later stages and on the day before the cease-fire, the majority was . . . in favor of the action we had taken to the extent of about four to one. . . .
> The little I saw of public demonstrations confirmed this. Every day I drove in the early afternoon across to the House of Commons. . . . In the early days the booing about equalled the cheering. As time went on, the booing grew fainter and the cheering louder until in the last stages the booing had entirely disappeared; except in the House of Commons.[89]

Eden believed that the renewed Egyptian resistance in Port Said, after the local Egyptian commander had agreed to surrender to the Anglo-French force on the afternoon of November 5

> . . . was prompted from further afield. We may never be able to prove it, but what is certain and significant is that loudspeaker vans toured Port Said announcing that Russian

help was on the way, that London and Paris had been bombed and that the third world war had started. At this moment a menacing letter from Bulganin had been dispatched to me, the first word I had received from him since our decision to intervene. *Encouraged by the attitude of the United States* and the United Nations, the Russians had taken their decision. The Soviet Consul became suddenly active in Port Said, stimulating resistance and promising help. The Russian hat was now in the ring. . . .

Their first intervention at the Security Council [had been] more moderate than that of the United States and did not condemn Anglo-French action as Mr. Cabot Lodge's resolution had done. Their propaganda was stepped up only some days after it became clear that the United States was in the lead against us at the United Nations. Oblivious of Hungary, the Russians felt they could snarl with the pack. . . .

Probably they were suspicious that official United States indignation against its allies could not really be as violent as it appeared. From the Soviet angle it was rather too good to be true. To them it seemed *unthinkable that the United States should not be as mindful of the interests of its allies as Soviet Russia was prepared to be of hers.*[90]

For Eden and his Cabinet, the most menacing feature in the situation now was not the vulgarly phrased Soviet threat of reprisals by rocket attack against Britain, though this "caused scare headlines in some sections of the press"— doubtless the same organs that a year later were eagerly anticipating a British disaster in the operations in Oman.[91] The most serious danger was the rapid depletion of Britain's gold and dollar reserves, "made immediately critical by speculation against sterling, largely in the American market or on American account," which "could have been decisive within the next few days."[92] Thus Eden and his colleagues decided to defer to the U.S.-U.S.S.R.-U.N. consensus.

> There is every reason to believe that the cease-fire was
> ordered not willingly but with great reluctance; not because
> the objective had been achieved nor because of vague threats
> from Russia, which were safely ignored, but under pressure
> from a United States Government which had not hesitated to
> use against Great Britain those sanctions which it had refused
> to invoke against Egypt.[93]

In addition, the United States Government "had used every
resource at their command" to induce Israel to accept the
cease-fire:

> There were promises also. President Eisenhower sent a
> personal appeal to Mr. Ben-Gurion in which he declared
> that once Israel had withdrawn from Egyptian territory new
> and energetic steps would be taken to solve the basic prob-
> lems which had given rise to the present difficulty. . . .
> We had not understood that, so far from doing this, the
> United Nations, and in particular the United States, would
> insist that all the advantages gained must be thrown away
> before serious negotiation began. This was the most calam-
> itous of all errors. Had we expected it to be perpetrated, our
> course might have been otherwise. . . .
> In the months after these events [Eden writes] I repeat-
> edly read and heard the comment, especially from the United
> States, even from those in high authority: "If only you had
> gone on."[94]

On the afternoon of November 6, Eden was telephoned
by President Eisenhower:

> He was vigorous and in good spirits. He was delighted
> by our order to cease fire and commented that we had got
> what we had set out to do; the fighting was over and had
> not spread. Mr. Eisenhower was naturally elated by the
> Presidential election results. . . .

The President followed his telephone call with a telegram. It was cordial in tone, but contained some indications
of the direction of American thinking which I was perhaps
slow to recognize. I did not foresee then that the United
States Government would harden against us on almost every
point and become harsher after the cease-fire than before. . . .

In spite of the President's exchanges with me [Eden
continues], we were not sure that his Administration understood the true situation in the area. At lower levels our
warnings had been ignored. Our immediate purpose must be
to resume close relations with the United States and induce
them to recognize the real dangers of Soviet penetration. . . .

I thought that there should be an immediate consultation
with Mr. Eisenhower and M. Mollet. . . . On the 7th I followed the President's suggestion and telephoned to him. The
President was receptive. I told him I thought it was important that we should meet and have a full discussion on the
situation. He agreed and asked me what date I had in mind.
I said the sooner the better and suggested that M. Mollet
and I might fly over that evening. . . . The President author-
ized me to invite M. Mollet . . . and to tell him that a con-
firmatory invitation from the President would follow. . . .

About an hour later the President telephoned to me and
said he wanted to be clear that I was not making the journey
just to argue about the United Nations resolutions. . . . I
assured him that was not my purpose.

Later he telephoned again and said that he would be
much taken up in the days ahead in consultations with the
leaders of Congress. He had come to the conclusion, therefore, that M. Mollet and I should defer our visit, though he
did not rule it out for a later date. . . .

Later that evening I sent the President a telegram. . . .

The President replied agreeing to a meeting at an early
date, but he held that the United Nations resolutions must
be carried out. This meant that the Anglo-French forces

should be withdrawn from Egypt without delay. Mr. Eisenhower now considered that the ground would be favorable
for a meeting only when this had been done. Thus we and
the French were squarely asked to give up the gage we had
won, before concerting with the United States any common
policy for the Middle East.[95]

This led to a new deadlock, since the British and French
Governments were determined to keep their troops in the
Canal Zone until the international force was there in strength:
"We had to avoid a vacuum between our departure and the
arrival of a sufficient United Nations force." Meanwhile, in
that longer stretch of the Suez Canal in which they had not
lost control:

> . . . the Egyptians were busy sinking ships. By far the greater
> part of this obstruction to the Canal was done after the
> fighting was over, when politically and physically it was safe
> to do so. By the time the Egyptians had finished, they had
> sunk thirty-two ships in the Canal, while their propaganda
> was busy blaming the Allied bombing for their own act of
> sabotage. . . . The United States showed no signs of readiness
> to assist France and Britain with oil supplies from the West-
> ern hemisphere.
>
> The Egyptian Government took instant advantage of this
> situation and from a position of weakness were once again
> allowed to seize a position of strength. They declared that
> they would not contemplate the clearance of the Canal until
> after the Anglo-French forces had gone. . . . Under this
> Egyptian pressure the United Nations gave way. Even before
> Mr. Hammarskjöld paid his visit to Cairo on November 16th,
> he had largely accepted the Egyptian point of view. . . .
>
> At this juncture the Foreign Secretary flew to New York
> where he remained for ten days, struggling to inject some
> sense of values. His efforts were largely wasted. The Presi-

dent a few days earlier had granted a friendly interview to
our new Ambassador. . . . [He] said he had differed sharply
with us on tactics, but he shared my [Eden's] views on Colonel Nasser. He agreed that the urgent task ahead was to
work out a settlement of both the Suez and the Arab-Israeli
problems. These were promising words, but the President's
attitude was not reflected in the actions of his Administration. Mr. Dulles at this time was ill and the authorities in
charge of the State Department during his absence[96] were
aggressively negative when the Foreign Secretary urged our
views upon them. In the possession of Port Said and the
Israeli occupation of Sinai, we held strong bargaining coun-
ters. Before we agreed to relinquish them, we must ensure
that the Canal was promptly cleared and that a general settlement of the problems of the area was under negotiation.
Soviet designs for penetrating the Middle East had gone
much further than the United States believed.[97] . . .

When the Foreign Secretary used these arguments, he
was met with expressions of moral disapproval. . . . The
United States officials refused to cooperate at any level of
policy-making. They declared that Britain, France and the
United States must not appear to be conspiring together
behind the back of the United Nations. Their only reaction
to reports of Russian infiltration in the Middle East was to
press us to remove our forces more quickly.

We could not help contrasting the American attitude
now with our own attitude at the time of the Guatemala
campaign [1954]. In that country the United States had
encouraged the overthrow of a Communist-influenced Government. . . . We had understood their action there and
done what we could not to hamper them in the Security
Council. They were now behaving in a precisely contrary
manner towards us. When this point was put to the United
States officials, they had no answer.[98] . . .

The attitude was rather that the President had been

slighted because the Allies had acted without permission. The Allies must pay for it. . . . The many warnings, both public and private, which had been given by the Allies over the waiting months did not help to assuage official American opinion. On the contrary, they irritated it. . . .

The President had indefinitely postponed consultation with M. Mollet and myself. He did not receive the Foreign Secretary in Washington, nor the Australian Foreign Minister . . . who was the bearer of a message from the Australian Prime Minister.[99] The United States Administration seemed to be dominated at this time by one thought only, to harry their allies. Mr. Dulles, who was still recovering from an operation,[100] *deplored to the Foreign Secretary that we had not managed to bring Nasser down and declared that he must be prevented from getting away with it.* The actions of the United States Government had exactly the opposite result.[101]

Before the meeting of the U.N. General Assembly in plenary session on November 23, Eden reports:

President Eisenhower once more proclaimed in public that he wished to strengthen the Anglo-American alliance. Armed with this authority, the Foreign Secretary and [British] Ambassador in Washington both renewed their exchanges with high American officials. We were allies in NATO and SEATO, the present Soviet threat was directed at the Middle East, which lay between the spheres of these two pacts. We could hardly be allies in two parts of the world and not in a third. These efforts got us nowhere. One senior American authority frankly declared that it was not possible at this stage for the Administration to talk to Her Majesty's Government. We were accused of "stalling" on the resolutions of the United Nations and we were taxed with having created the "black-out" between our countries. . . .

The United States Administration continued obstinately silent, so the Foreign Secretary and his French colleague returned home. The Arab-Israeli problem remained unsolved. The Canal was handed back to the control of one man, who was picked up, dusted down and put in full authority again. . . . Western Europe would be naïve indeed to expect free passage of the Canal at any time of emergency, unless it has the power to compel it, which it is not likely to have again. . . .

The United States could not have taken up so legalistic an attitude if the security of its own continent had been at stake.[102]

In the words of a reviewer in *The Guardian* (Manchester) on February 29, 1960:

Others may hold that, with different tactics from the end of July onwards, the Canal could have been brought under international control and the American alliance kept intact. The United Nations could have been strengthened, and it would then have been better able to cope with the Hungarian crisis. The pull of Arab nationalism need not have been so much in Nasser's favor; and in Iraq something could have been saved from the wreck.

But this piece of wishful thinking ignored the fact that Eden's most vehement critics in the English-speaking countries had positively applauded "the pull of Arab nationalism . . . in Nasser's favor" and/or were complacent about the subsequent "dismemberment" of Iraq's pro-Western Prime Minister by a Baghdad mob.[103] Far more percipient was the American reviewer who remarked, "It is conceivable that the Dulles subtlety and deviousness might have found a better way through the Middle Eastern problem; but Eden was at least the man who *did* something about it."[104] In the words of another American reviewer:

> John Foster Dulles had his hour of triumph. But had he won? Eighteen months later American and British forces entered the Lebanon and Jordan to preserve the peace. Was there a whisper then in Mr. Dulles's mind of something similar in the recent past? Probably not. Mr. Dulles seldom appreciated the ironies of history, especially when he was making it.[105]

Eden, on the other hand, underlines the ironical fact that the U.S. and British interventions in 1958 ignored the "myopic testimony" of the U.N. observers who reported that they could not find evidence of subversive activity by Egypt and Syria.[106] The Anglo-American action, says Eden in language partly paralleled by Dulles, ". . . was necessary if the right to live of these two small countries was to be preserved; it was unquestionably against the terms of the Charter as interpreted at the time of our intervention at Port Said."[107]

All that immediately issued from the U.S. Government's mountainous travail over Suez was the *ridiculus mus* of the Eisenhower Doctrine, on which *The Times* (London) commented as follows on January 7, 1957:

> It is easy to say that it comes very late, that it is fearfully vague in parts, and that it is largely irrelevant to the main causes of the Middle Eastern upheavals, tensions, and dangers. . . . Far and away the greatest advantage . . . springs from the new and keener interest which the President is impelling Congress to take in the Middle East. The story of last year would not have been so erratic and agonizing for Britain and France if such concern had been shown by Washington then. By asking Congress to authorize in advance the use of American forces in case of Communist or

Communist-controlled aggression, the President has given Congress and American public opinion the severest of prods. Far too often last year Americans tended to think that the future of the Suez Canal and of the oilfields was something for Britain and France to worry about, but not for America.[108] . . .

Against these advantages must be set many weaknesses and obscurities. First and foremost, it would be calamitous if Congress, stung into interest, became interested in the Middle East in the wrong way. We should all be worse off if American opinion were . . . to concentrate on the danger of open Communist aggression and to ignore all the urgent strains—the rivalries between Arab states themselves, the hostility of all Arab states to Israel, the future of the oil companies and the oil pipelines, Egypt's ambitions and Nasser's arrogance.

Insisting in February, 1957, that Israel should withdraw her forces from the localities they had occupied during the Sinai campaign, President Eisenhower said: "We should not assume that, if Israel withdraws, Egypt will prevent Israeli shipping from using the Suez Canal. . . . If, unhappily, Egypt does hereafter violate the armistice agreement [of 1949] or other international obligations, then this should be dealt with firmly by the society of nations."[109] The Egyptian regime did, however, remain obdurate on this point, and the persuasion of the U.N. Secretary-General on repeated occasions was ineffectual in bringing about any change. In 1960, another Presidential election year in the United States, President Eisenhower admitted his own impotence at a press conference on April 27: "Mr. Nasser has given as his reason for doing nothing . . . that they are in a state of war. . . . Now, I don't know what you can do unless you want to resort to force in such affairs, and I'm certain that we're not trying to settle international

problems with force. . . . I don't know that there is any idea
whatsoever of making a new step in this direction or new
argument because I think it's all been said." This continuing
sterility of thought with regard to the free use of the Suez
Canal was the natural consequence of the "great divorce" in
Anglo-American policy which has been the subject of this
chapter. The fundamental error committed by Eden and the
British conservatives (*quorum pars minima ego*) was to imagine the relationship between the two leading governments of
the English-speaking peoples as a "marriage of true minds,"
with an element of give and take which would operate in
Britain's favor in the Middle East, where she had been the
leading power for 150 years and the U.S. interest had developed only during the past 20 years.[110] But the hard fact, as a
veteran pro-Zionist colonel saw it, was that "So far as America
is concerned, Britain is just an island in the Atlantic, a recipi-
ent of charity and a convenient outpost."[111] Or, as an American
commentator put it more tactfully, Eden had failed to grasp
"what the emergence of the United States as a world power
really meant to Britain and her place in the world."[112] Eden
mentions a report, considered reliable by the British Embassy
in Washington, that Dulles had told U.S. journalists in 1954
that U.S. policy in the Middle East "had been badly handi-
capped by a tendency to support British and French 'colonial'
views. He was reported to have spoken of his determination
to talk bluntly about the Middle East, and of his aim to 'shift
policies.' "[113] In the Suez crisis, impatience with Washington's
readiness to let things "drift" and with its spinsterish fastidious-
ness for Anglo-French interests and methods[114] had led the
British and French Governments into their ill-fated "declaration of independence" in the Middle East. This threw the U.S.
Government once again into an unnatural temporary association with the U.S.S.R.,[115] and British and French influences

were thereby almost wholly ousted from the Levant for the time being. The way thus lay open for the emancipated State Department eventually to make a new experiment in international living with Abdel Nasser[116]—an experiment that I was tempted at the beginning of 1960 to satirize under the irreverent but prophetic title of "Lady Chatterley's Poacher."

CHAPTER 5

THE SMOTHERING OF SYRIA

The overthrow of the Syrian military dictator Colonel Adib Shishakli early in 1954 was followed by a restoration of the Constitution of 1950. The well-to-do politicians who had been displaced by a military *coup d'état* after the disgrace of the Palestine War now returned to power and, in the elections held in the fall of 1954, secured 70 per cent of the seats in the Chamber. But just as in the elections held under the French mandate a minority of "extreme" nationalists had often been able to dominate a Chamber composed of mainly disorganized moderates,[1] so now the political tone was set by a radical group, the Arab Socialist Resurrection (Ba'th) Party, although its sixteen deputies constituted only 11 per cent of the Chamber. This party was the result of a recent compromise between the radical principles of Michel Aflaq, an ideologue with Christian parents and a French secular education, and the adroit political opportunism of Akram Hawrani, who as a fellow townsman of Colonel Shishakli had hoped to be his political mentor. Finding himself increasingly disregarded by Shishakli, however, Hawrani had escaped to Beirut, there to plot with Aflaq and the third member of the Ba'th triumvirate, Salah ud-Din Bitar. These men, all about forty years of age, had drawn up a program of Arab unity and social-economic radicalism, directed especially against foreign concessionaires and the great landlords—a program that naturally appealed to those younger urban "intellectuals," including some army officers, who saw no great prospects for themselves under a regime of the conservative politicians. As in Iraq after the overthrow of the military dictator Bakr Sidqi in 1937, the return to constitutionalism had not led to any lessening of political intrigue within the army;[2] and the influence of the Ba'th therein was contested by a rival radical party, al-Hizb al-Qawmi al-Ijtima'i,[3] whose differences with the Ba'th perhaps turned, in the last analysis, more on personalities than on principles.[4] The Ba'th had a strong point of influence with the army in the Deputy Chief of Staff, Colonel Adnan al-Maliki; but in the course of a series of conflicts between the Ba'th and its opponents in various towns early in 1955, this officer was shot dead by a member of al-Hizb al-Qawmi. This party was thereupon outlawed, and some scores of its members were brought to trial. Three of the most prominent ones were given death sentences (at the same time, five more were similarly condemned *in absentia*); after being taken to the appeal court, these sentences went to the President of the Republic for confirmation. However, the conservative Shukri al-Kuwatly (whose re-election to that office in 1955 had been opposed by the Ba'th) was reluctant to seal this factional fighting with the finality of the gallows; and the Syrian political scene in mid-1956 was thus a precarious balance between the conservatives, among whom was the new Chief of Staff, Brigadier Nizām ud-Dīn, and the Ba'th, which now held the portfolios of Foreign Affairs and National Economy, as well as the important post of head of Military Intelligence in the person of the thirty-two-year-old Major Abdul Hamid Serraj.[5]

The Egyptian military junta led by Gamal Abdel Nasser

had a "material power" which the Ba'th lacked, while the
Ba'th believed it could furnish Nasser with its ideology in the
common struggle for Arab unity.[6] The international crisis
which followed the Egyptian expropriation of the Suez Canal
Company accordingly found both the Ba'th and the Syrian
conservatives (forced by necessity)[7] staunchly supporting
Egypt. The Syrian Government had followed Egypt in establishing closer relations with the U.S.S.R. and in recognizing
Communist China; and on October 30, 1956, the very day
of the Anglo-French ultimatum to Egypt and Israel which
precipitated the Suez crisis, President Kuwatly left Damascus
on a three-day visit to Moscow. The Syrian Government proclaimed its complete solidarity with Egypt in meeting the
Anglo-French-Israeli "aggression" against her; and in the first
days of November, the pumping stations on the IPC oil pipeline crossing Syrian territory were blown up—by units of the
Syrian Army, according to IPC information.[8]

On November 21, after the cease-fire on the Egyptian
front and while the U.N. General Assembly was debating the
Hungarian question, the Syrian delegate asked the Assembly
to pay immediate attention to "an imminent Anglo-French-
Israeli aggression against Syria," of which no confirmation was
forthcoming. Four days later, the Syrian press published the
following communiqué from a military spokesman:

> At the moment when the forces of iniquity and of Anglo-
> French-Jewish aggression were attacking our valiant Egyp-
> tian brothers with a ferocity unparalleled in the history of
> mankind, and at the critical moment when all the units of
> the Syrian Army were on the move, eager to make their
> national contribution to the struggle for existence and honor
> at the side of the Egyptian and Jordanian units as brother-
> hood and the identity of our cause and destiny required—
> just at this critical moment, the Syrian military authorities

came into possession of great quantities of important war material during an attempt to transfer it into Syria from a neighboring Arab country. Thereupon an investigation was begun, and the culprits arrested who were preparing to stab in the back their nation, their fatherland, and their army as they stood ready to engage themselves in the fight.

The first pieces of evidence revealed those with whom these lawbreakers were in league. We say with anguished mind and bleeding heart that it was a government on which we relied until recently to place itself at our side in the day of battle, in spite of its having taken the wrong road and been deceived by the policy of alliances and the imperialists.

We assure all our fellow countrymen, sons of this Arab people in Syria, that her responsible sons who have the evidence before them will act with all devotion and energy to lay their hands upon all the accomplices and participants, to bring them before the courts and judge them, so that their base crime against the nation, the fatherland, the people, and the army may receive its fitting punishment.

As for that government of Nuri as-Sa'id in Iraq that has incited these lawbreakers to plot against us on behalf of the enemy and Israel, it is beyond doubt that its account will be settled by the valiant Arab people it has scorned—that people which does not lack energy but has always been heroic and glorious, from the times of the caliphs al-Walid and ar-Rashid down to the day of the national struggle that is now upon us. Its hour has sounded, and the skirmishing has begun."

In the first half of December, a National Parliamentary Front, pledged *inter alia* to see justice done against those involved in this conspiracy, was formed under the leadership of the Ba'th and rapidly grew to include more than half the members of the Chamber. The conservative Sha'b Party, consisting mainly of well-to-do citizens of Aleppo and Homs, re-

mained outside this Front, and on December 22 Prime Minister Sabri al-Atasi re-formed his Cabinet to exclude its former
Sha'b members. On the same day, it was announced that
among those awaiting trial for complicity in the alleged conspiracy were a number of ex-ministers and other notables of
the Sha'b Party, together with tribal sheikhs, members of the
proscribed party al-Hizb al-Qawmi, and relatives and supporters of ex-dictator Shishakli. The Iraqi Foreign Minister
and Deputy Chief of Staff were alleged to have furnished
money and arms for the purpose of overthrowing the present
Syrian Government and replacing it with one more friendly
to Iraq;[10] Lebanese members of al-Hizb al-Qawmi were said
to be implicated, as well as the British Military Attaché in
Beirut. The trial opened on January 8, 1957, in the largest
public hall in Damascus, and not only the setting but the
confessions of the accused were reminiscent of the political
trials held in the "people's democracies" which the Ba'th
seemed determined to emulate in their country.[11] The hearings
ended five weeks later, and the sentences were pronounced on
February 27: five death sentences, later commuted to penal
servitude for life, and the rest long sentences of imprisonment. On the same day, thirty members of al-Hizb al-Qawmi
were indicted on charges of inciting violent demonstrations
at Aleppo against the government.

Despite these charges and the circumstantial evidence of
widespread conspiracy against the Syrian state, political circles
continued to be far from united in the face of the alleged peril.
It was reported in March that the more conservative segments of the Cabinet and the army had attempted—though
to no purpose—to obtain the transfer of Colonel Serraj and
a large number of his radical following of young officers.[12]
The conservative counterrevolution carried out in April by
King Husain in Jordan, with the support of the Saudi and

United States Governments,[13] brought to Syria scores of Jordanian political refugees sympathetic to the Ba'th Party, and Akram Hawrani himself addressed strong recriminations to the Saudi Deputy Foreign Minister when he visited Damascus at the end of June.[14] At that time, an American journalist estimated the value of Soviet war material supplied to Syria during the past fifteen months at $150-200 million, and reported as follows on the regimentation of public opinion:

> Only seven of the country's twenty-nine dailies . . . take an uncompromisingly Communist line. But the others are forced to rely heavily on what the Egyptians and the Russians see fit to tell them.
>
> Egyptian dailies sell almost as widely here as Syrian, and Egyptian weeklies far more widely. The Egyptian news agency MENA provides the bulk of all published news. The Egyptian newsreel *Misr* has been distributed free to all movie houses by the Syrian Office of Propaganda for the past year, thus driving all Western newsreels out of the market. Radio Cairo is picked up by the Syrian radio within fifteen minutes of a broadcast, and during the Suez crisis . . . two Egyptians were stationed at Syrian radio headquarters to direct handling of commentaries and news.
>
> The Russians, for their part, have covered Syrian newsstands with attractive publications in Arabic and French. Their news agency, Tass, has a large office in Damascus headed by a thoroughly trained Arabist, who issues two daily bulletins and often provides special services. Russian films and documentaries are shown in at least one first-run movie house each week. Radio Moscow is quoted almost as frequently as Radio Cairo, and the Soviet Embassy—with a much more elaborate diplomatic staff than any other in Damascus—has been so diligent and generous about placing "cultural" stories in the Syrian press that it has made many local editors prosperous, if not rich. . . .

"The Russians don't have to ask us to do anything," says a leader of one of the anti-Communist parties. "We will do anything we think they *might* want, we are so grateful."[15]

The Syrian authorities claimed to have arrested on June 8 three members of an espionage organization providing the British with military and political information on Syria;[16] and on July 1, a Damascus newspaper announced the discovery of a United States plot to subvert the Syrian Government. The U.S. Ambassador and Military Attaché in Damascus were alleged to have organized the smuggling of arms into Syria from Turkey, Iraq, and Lebanon with the complicity of the Iraqi Deputy Chief of Staff (already cited in the conspiracy of the previous winter), Syrian fugitives (also involved in that conspiracy), and leaders of the recent Jordanian counter-revolution. All this, and more, was said to have been confirmed to an Arab diplomat by the head of the Syrian desk in the U.S. Department of State![17] After visiting Damascus, the assistant editor of the *New Statesman* reported that since the adoption by Washington of the Eisenhower Doctrine for the Middle East, U.S. Intelligence was alleged to have been in contact with the Syrian senior field commanders under the Chief of Staff, General Nizām ud-Dīn, who were opposed to the radical policy followed by Serraj and the Ba'th.[18] On August 13, the Syrian Government requested the immediate departure of the Military Attaché of the U.S. Embassy, of a Second Secretary, and of a Vice-Consul. They were accused of plotting with al-Hizb al-Qawmi and members of the armed forces to overthrow the government.[19] Ten Syrian officers were placed on the retired list, and the Chief of Staff was replaced by Brigadier Afif al-Bizri, an alleged Communist. The U.S. Government replied by declaring the Syrian Ambassador to Washington *persona non grata,* and a State Department offi-

cial told the press that the Syrian tactics—of making un-
founded charges that the U.S. had plotted to overthrow the
Syrian Government and then subjecting the U.S. Embassy to
the oppressive "protection" of a cordon of thirty to forty
Syrian troops—was "the type of thing that has gone on in
Czechoslovakia, Hungary, and other areas" controlled by the
U.S.S.R.[20] On September 7, Secretary Dulles gave an account
of the findings of one of his Assistant Secretaries, Loy Henderson, who in the latter half of August had been sent as a
special representative of the President to confer with the Turkish, Iraqi, Jordanian, and Lebanese Governments. He had
found ". . . deep concern at the apparently growing Soviet
Communist domination of Syria and the large build-up there
of Soviet-bloc arms . . . which could not be justified by purely
defensive needs. There was particular concern over border
incidents and intensive propaganda and subversive activities
directed toward the overthrow of the newly constituted governments of Syria's Arab neighbors." This seemed to refer
particularly to King Husain's regime in Jordan, and a supply
of U.S. war materials was sent to that country by air transport
to accelerate the existing program.[21] There were warnings from
friendly diplomatic circles that these U.S. moves (which had
the "full support" of the British Foreign Office) might have
the effect of hardening the Syrian attitude; Syrian and Egyptian official spokesmen confirmed that the consolidation of
the influence of the young radical Syrian army officers had
strengthened the relations between their two countries; and
on September 10, Dulles moderated the tension that had
arisen, expressing the belief that the situation would probably
work out peacefully.[22]

On the same day that Dulles made this pacifying statement, Soviet Premier Bulganin wrote to the Turkish Prime
Minister:

The Soviet Government cannot conceal its concern about the Syrian situation. It is well-known that Syria and Egypt, while following their policy of national independence, have been exposed for some time to hostile political, economic, and military pressures from outside. In recent weeks the pressure on Syria has risen to a dangerous height. The recent journey of the American envoy Henderson to the Middle East clearly reveals the intention to organize a foreign armed intervention in the internal affairs of Syria. It is known that Henderson's task was to arrange a plot against Syria, studying the means of bringing down its national government and changing the whole balance of the country to please the great American monopolies and the interests of the chief imperialist powers.

In this connection the imperialist states openly declare that Turkey has a definite role to play in the military operations to be undertaken against Syria. . . .

We have received with great alarm the news of Turkish military concentrations on the Syrian border, and of the sending of American arms to Turkey for organizing attacks on Syria. . . .

The U.S.S.R. cannot regard all these recent developments with indifference. . . . The reports of Turkish concentrations on the Syrian border naturally raise the question: What would the Turks think if foreign troops were concentrated on *their* border? We are certain that the Turks would bitterly regret having followed the advice of foreign circles who are not in the least interested in maintaining the peace of the Middle East, but are solely concerned with exploiting its natural resources. We are convinced that, if war should break out in Syria and spread to the Middle East, Turkey would have everything to lose by taking part in it.[23]

A month later, Khrushchev, in an interview with James Reston of *The New York Times,* addressed far blunter threats to Turkey, and in mid-October the Syrian and Soviet Governments asked the U.N. General Assembly to investigate the alleged Turkish preparations (allegedly supported by the United States) for an attack on Syria. The Syrian Army whipped up what seems to have been a largely artificial war scare, organizing all students (including girls) for military training, ordering practice in street fighting, the digging of trenches, and the raising of roadblocks on all approaches to the city of Aleppo, thirty miles from the Turkish border. An offer of mediation by King Saud was at first accepted by the conservative Syrian President, but (apparently under pressure from the radical officers) he then asked the King to withdraw the offer. No resolution emerged from the General Assembly debate, and by the end of the year there were suggestions ". . . that a behind-the-scene struggle is going on in Damascus between full Sovietists and those who are glad to use Soviet aid but are wary of becoming subservient to Moscow, and who see the advantage of Soviet support to exact better conditions from the West."[24] Among those most ready to flirt with the U.S.S.R., besides the Chief of Staff (Colonel Bizri), was the Minister of Defense and (since mid-November) of Finance, Khalid al-'Azm. This aristocratic landowner had served the Vichy French administration as chief of the Syrian state in 1941; but having been defeated by Kuwatly in the presidential election of 1955, he had made an opportunistic turn to the left and had successfully negotiated arms and trade deals with the U.S.S.R. during a visit to Moscow in the summer of 1957; on December 9, he became Deputy Prime Minister, in addition to the two portfolios he already held. The Ba'th leaders, having disposed of al-Hizb al-Qawmi, their rivals, and having intimidated into submission the conservatives of the Sha'b and the National Parties, now apparently feared being outmaneuvered by a combination of the Communists with al-'Azm.[25] They therefore renewed the overtures they had made early in 1956 for a federation with Egypt. The Egyptian military junta, for its part, badly needed some new injection of prestige to offset its alienation of King Saud, the Lebanese Government's acceptance of the Eisenhower Doctrine and successful handling of the elections of June, 1957, and King Husain's successful counterrevolution.[26]

In mid-October, at the height of the war scare generated by the Turkish army maneuvers on the Syrian border, some two battalions of Egyptian troops had been sent to that border as a gesture of "solidarity." A month later, a visit to Syria by forty members of the Egyptian National Assembly (elected under the scrutiny of the military junta according to the authoritarian provisions of the constitution of 1956)[27] was made the occasion for a joint session with the Syrian Chamber headed by the Ba'th leader Akram Hawrani, who had been elected President of the Chamber in mid-October; a unanimous resolution invited the two governments to negotiate a federal union of the two countries. The Egyptian regime, however, seems to have been in no hurry to complete the transaction until in mid-January, 1958, President Kuwatly hurried to Cairo and persuaded Abdel Nasser that they should jointly announce the establishment of the United Arab Republic on February 1. Four days later, the Secretary of the Syrian Communist Party, Khalid Bakdash, accompanied by his family and eight other Party members, left Damascus for the U.S.S.R., and a plebiscite ratified this step toward Arab unity by the ritual majority of 99.9 per cent.

From the beginning, however, there was a latent contradiction between Abdel Nasser's subordination of all political activity to his "national union"[28] and his consequent dissolution of political parties in the newly acquired "northern province" as in Egypt itself, and the role which the Ba'th designed for itself as the future ruling party of the U.A.R.:

> The "national union" which Abdel Nasser planned for Syria was seen by the Ba'th only from the standpoint of its own interests. . . . Michel Aflaq had already declared that the Ba'th was providing Abdel Nasser with "a philosophy and an ideology." The president of the United Arab Republic was to be, in the last instance, merely the "secular arm" of the Ba'th for bringing into actuality its plans for the Arab world.[29]

The unexpected and, for Abdel Nasser, highly disconcerting turn taken by the Iraqi revolution in 1958-59[30] provided a pressing reason why he should seek to regulate this latent contradiction in Egyptian-Syrian relations within the U.A.R.:

> . . . in Egypt, a regime completely centered on the army and excluding any political organization that was not military; in Syria, an authority deriving from the association of a civilian party, the Ba'th, and the army. The two-man rule of Akram Hawrani and Abdul Hamid Serraj, which had made some sense while Syria was still nominally under a parliamentary regime, no longer had any *raison d'être*.
>
> From the establishment of the U.A.R., the struggle between the Syrian military boss [Serraj] and the leader of the Ba'th [Hawrani] was unavoidable and practically an open one. And it followed logically that it should be the Ba'th, as a state within a state, that paid the price. Its eventual fate followed from its having, ever since 1954, pursued a policy that had alienated from it the sympathies of a large section of public opinion.[31]

This loss of popularity was aggravated by an external factor, the adverse economic effect of two successive winters of drought, during 1957-59. The occasion for a showdown between the U.A.R. ruling junta and the Ba'th was the local elections for delegates to the "national union," held in July, 1959:

> It was a new proof of Abdel Nasser's adroitness that he did not himself repudiate the party that he had called to power, but let the Syrians do it. Very skillfully the leader and Serraj decided that the elections on July 8 should be as liberal and democratic as possible.
>
> Evidently the Syrians took full advantage of this atmosphere of freedom to which they thought they had said goodbye some time before. The election campaign aroused in the "northern province" a passionate interest which contrasted sharply with the apathy and resignation of the Egyptian rank and file. In a sort of general opposition movement the old parties and groups re-formed their ranks and put forward lists of coalition candidates designed for the most part to oppose the Ba'th. The latter was compelled to carry out a strategic withdrawal from most of the electoral districts on account of the systematic obstruction which it encountered. Almost everywhere in Syria there were demonstrations against Hawrani's party . . . [while Hawrani himself was evidently detained in Cairo in his role as Vice President of the U.A.R. and was not allowed to go to Syria for the elections].[32]

The Ba'th having thus been permitted to win only 250 seats out of the 9,445 allotted to the "Syrian province," the next stage in Syria's submergence in the Egyptian tide was Abdel Nasser's appointment of his faithful Egyptian acolyte, Abdul Hākim Āmir (already titular commander-in-chief of the armed forces of the U.A.R.), as *Gauleiter* of Syria, with the executive ministers of the "Syrian province" made responsible to him in all respects.[33] One immediate cause for this appointment was reported to be clashes between Syrian and Egyptian army officers in which at least two Egyptian officers had been killed by Syrians.[34] Nevertheless, Āmir wished it to appear that his appointment was solely for the purpose of speeding up Syria's internal development: "We must drive to make Syrian social and economic progress catch up with that of Egypt"—a pregnant statement for those who knew how much the economic progress of independent Syria had been ahead of Egypt's.[35] With equal blandness, Āmir ". . . denied flatly there was any trouble in the Syrian Army resulting from the appointment of some Egyptian officers to Syrian commands. 'The number of Syrian officers serving in the Egyptian Army in Egypt is much greater than the number of Egyptian officers in the Syrian Army,' he declared. In fact, the Field Marshal continued, the Syrians are demanding more Egyptian officers."[36] Abdul Hamid Serraj remained *in situ* as Minister of the Interior and Director of Propaganda and Information; but at the end of the year, Akram Hawrani and four other Ba'th ministers resigned from the central cabinet of the U.A.R. (or the provincial cabinet), and a month later three more Syrians likewise left the central cabinet. It was surmised that reports of skirmishing between the Syrian and Israeli forces on the border in the upper Jordan valley were perhaps exaggerated in order to camouflage the ensuing cabinet reshuffle; and at the end of May, a special correspondent could report:

> From behind their desks the Egyptians and their Syrian colleagues can now contemplate the prospect with more equanimity than after the Field Marshal's appointment last October as President Nasser's pro-consul in the "northern region." As evidence of a better situation, a senior officer cited a "three-quarters reduction" in the business handled by the complaints bureau: in the first four months after its establishment by Marshal Āmir it was contending with a flood of 3,000 letters daily.

"They're now speaking about economics instead of politics," said the officer with evident satisfaction. The Syrian armed forces, he indicated, were now quiet—after the transfer of the more restless elements to Egypt. . . . Air travel between Cairo and Damascus is costly enough to prevent a Syrian on duty in Egypt from coming home for the weekend.

While, considering the well-known touchiness of the Syrian character, there can be no certain guarantee against sudden turbulence, the country as a whole now seems to be entering a period of increased stability. Economically, a proper development plan is being embarked upon, in conjunction with a thorough study of problems and potentialities. Politically, the Ba'thists . . . are unhappy and divided as well as disorganized. Such Communists as have not been incarcerated by Colonel Serraj's all-powerful security corps have been pushed deep underground.[37]

In September, Serraj seemed to have acquired still wider powers through his appointment as President of the Executive Council of the "northern region"; but at the same time Abdel Nasser amnestied five Syrian former politicians and one former army officer who had been among those caught in Serraj's intelligence net in 1957 and convicted of alleged conspiracy.[38]

CHAPTER 6

JORDANIA PHOENIX

The position of Glubb Pasha (afterwards Sir John Bagot Glubb) as Chief of Staff of the Jordanian Army had naturally long been obnoxious to Arab nationalists, both civilian and military.[1] The defection to the Egyptians of Lt. Col. Abdullah at-Tall, his accusation that King Abdullah and Glubb had jointly betrayed the Arab cause to the Israelis during the Palestine War, and at-Tall's probable complicity in the murder of King Abdullah in 1951 were, according to Glubb, a consequence of Glubb's unwillingness to approve his further accelerated promotion.[2] Later, young King Husain, after his accession to the throne, had in 1954 been introduced to the night life of Paris by Ali Abu Nuwar, a young officer and member of the Syrian Ba'th Party who had been appointed Jordanian Military Attaché to France to get him out of the way after his rash political talk had been reported.[3] In the fall of 1955, the young King had insisted on appointing Abu Nuwar as his chief aide-de-camp. That winter, the nationalist and left-wing forces in Jordan, egged on by Egyptian propaganda[4] and Saudi gold, held violent and destructive demonstrations when it was rumored that Jordan would join the Baghdad Pact.[5] The young King had considered such a move

107

as a means of obtaining increased military aid from Britain,[6] and had accordingly received a visit from the Chief of the Imperial General Staff. As a result of the violence, the King had dropped the idea, and Abu Nuwar and five other young officers evidently impressed upon him that his own position was in danger if he did not get rid of Glubb and terminate the treaty with Britain. Accordingly, on March 1, 1956, Glubb was given two hours' notice (afterwards graciously extended to eighteen) to leave the country he had served for the past twenty-six years. Two months later, Abu Nuwar was appointed Chief of Staff in his place, with the rank of Major-General, and a widespread purge was instituted of conservative Arab officers, who were replaced by members of Abu Nuwar's faction.

In June, 1956, the Parliament—which had been elected in 1954 with considerable government discrimination against the Ba'th and the National Socialist Party led by Sulaiman an-Nabulsi[7]—was dissolved, and preparations were made for a free general election in October. Meanwhile, Abu Nuwar:

> . . . was busy advancing the scheme, drawn up in Egypt, by which the Jordan army would accept an Egyptian Commander in the event of hostilities with Israel, and the King toured his western frontier, encouraging the overwrought people to a point where they fondly imagined that their day of deliverance [from Israel] was at hand.
>
> Whatever were Egypt's intentions, Jordan's young leaders at this time were allowing themselves to seem committed far beyond the lengths they really wanted to go. Even amongst the extremists the talk of war was largely political play-acting and those who talked loudest believed they could do so safely because, in the words of one of them, "Britain would prevent a war." . . . If Israel accepted Arab threats at their face value it was not unreasonable to do so. Egypt

appeared to mean business and to intend that Jordan should
be at the business end of the business. . . . In September, as
the screw seemed to tighten, Israel struck out, inflicting on
Jordan the deadliest blows in the whole history of frontier
clashes between them.[8]

In October, the British Government warned Israel that an
appeal from Jordan might bring the Anglo-Jordanian Treaty
into operation against her.[9] An offer of military support from
Nuri as-Sa'id, on the other hand, was not accepted by the
Jordan Government for fear that it might influence the forthcoming elections by provoking the pro-Egyptian factions.[10]

For the first time, the strongly nationalist parties won a
majority of the seats, the leading party being the National
Socialists, whose boss, Nabulsi, became Prime Minister and
appointed a leading Ba'th member, Abdullah ar-Rimawi, as
Foreign Minister. Three days later, on October 24, an agree-
ment was signed in Amman placing the Egyptian, Syrian, and
Jordanian armed forces under the joint command of the
Egyptian Commander-in-Chief. This appears to have been
the immediate cause for the Israeli mobilization and invasion
of Sinai, which precipitated the Anglo-French intervention.[11]
After the Suez crisis had subsided, the Jordanian and British
Governments agreed on the abrogation of their treaty, and
Saudi Arabia, Egypt, and Syria jointly undertook to provide
Jordan with the annual subsidy—now amounting to some
$35 million (12.5 million pounds sterling)—which Britain
had hitherto supplied, notably for Jordan's armed forces.

On April 10, 1957, however, King Husain called for the
resignation of Nabulsi's Cabinet, apparently because he disapproved of its recently announced intention of establishing
diplomatic relations for the first time with the U.S.S.R. and
of its numerous appointments of left-wing figures in public
positions. Nabulsi now formed his National Socialist Party,

the Ba'th, and other nationalists into a National Committee
to impose on the King a Cabinet of their choosing; but on
April 13, the King went out to the army camp at az-Zarqa
and rallied to his support part of the army (notably the
Bedouin troops) after a conflict with other troops supporting
Abu Nuwar and the leftists.[12] Returning to Amman, the King
ordered the dismissal and arrest of Abu Nuwar, who escaped,
however, to Syria with many other Ba'th officers and civilians.
Nabulsi, on the other hand, tried to organize an opposition
to the King from his native town of Nablus, and for a week
there were widespread strikes and riots which were repressed
by the heavy-handed Bedouin troops who were loyal to the
King but despised the townspeople. On April 24, the caretaker
Cabinet that had been formed was on the point of resigning,
but on that day the United States President and Secretary of
State issued a statement that they regarded "the independence
and integrity of Jordan as vital" to "the national interest and
world peace," as the Eisenhower Doctrine had specified. The
U.S. Sixth Fleet was ordered to the Eastern Mediterranean,
to the silent satisfaction of the British Foreign Office and the
dismay of those U.S. Congressmen who in January had regarded the Eisenhower Doctrine "as largely a moral and psychological effort unlikely to involve the U.S. in any grave
risk."[13] But, as a *New York Times* editorial pointed out, "Our
policy during the Suez crisis, when we said in effect, 'Let the
United Nations do it,' temporarily obscured the inescapable
demands of power politics and merely led to defeat for the
West."[14] The Egyptian military junta and the Syrian Ba'th,
aided and abetted by the U.S.S.R., had continued to exploit
this apparent Western weakness of purpose, and there was
thus *some* justification for King Husain's statement that the
propaganda campaign and the internal crisis in Jordan "were
the responsibility of international Communism and its fol-

lowers."[15] At least he had uttered the magic phrase that quieted American consciences (sensitive to the reproach that they might be acting like the unspeakable "men of Suez") and unloosed American purse strings. As Egypt and Syria defaulted in their undertaking to provide a financial subsidy to Jordan, the United States shouldered the obligation and, within two years, was aiding Jordan to the tune of some $70 million a year.

Thus, King Husain and his government of conservatives, with his army commanded once again by the Arab officers whom Glubb had trained, survived despite all the gloomy forecasts of the pessimists and the ill will of the Western partisans of "Arab unity" or Western retreat. The justification for supporting Jordan was that she provided a convenient buffer between the United Arab Republic, ostensibly eager for a "second round" in Palestine, and Israel, which might again be provoked into a preventive war;[16] but the pan-Arab conspirators were still at work in Damascus, and in August, 1960, the Jordanian Prime Minister and eleven other officials were killed by a bomb secreted in the Prime Minister's office.

CHAPTER 7

THE LEBANESE CIVIL WAR

Already, at the end of 1957, I had written of "the Syro-Egyptian campaign to harass Lebanon (the Middle Eastern 'Austria') into *Gleichschaltung*";[1] but I had not foreseen that these attempts would develop, in the course of 1958, into an international crisis comparable with that occasioned by the Spanish Civil War twenty years earlier. From the point of view of the pan-Arab nationalist, indeed, the existence of an independent Lebanon was as unnatural as the existence of an independent Austria was to the pan-German nationalist of the 1930's or earlier. Arabic was the language of the Lebanese people; and to use the Christian religion professed by approximately half their number as a reason for giving Lebanon sovereignty as a separate state seemed a survival of the sectarian considerations which the Arab nationalist claimed to repudiate. In fact, however, the region of Mount Lebanon had known a separate existence for centuries,[2] and its autonomy under a Christian governor had received international recognition in 1861. The French creation of *Grand Liban* in 1920 was not merely a piece of imperialist divide-and-rule technique, as Arab nationalists have since claimed, but also a concession to the territorial claims of a Lebanese Maronite

113

delegation that had presented its views to the Peace Conference of 1919.[3]

Lebanon stood out from the other Middle Eastern states, not in having minority communities of political importance, but in having no clear *majority* community as almost all other Middle Eastern countries had. The clear Christian majority of the former Sanjaq of Lebanon (1861-1914) was almost swamped by the extension of its boundaries into the *Grand Liban* of 1920. Even though the French had then conferred Lebanese citizenship on thousands of Armenian Christian refugees who had settled in the country after World War I, the census of 1932 showed a clear Christian majority only if large numbers from the extensive Lebanese diaspora abroad were included.[4] But the omission of the Armenians and the émigrés would not produce a clear Muslim majority either, as some superficial writers have supposed. The balance almost certainly lay with the Druze, who constituted 6 per cent of the population and whose peculiar religion was historically an offshoo. of Shi'i Islam but, like other heresies, had exposed them in the past to persecution by the majority community in Syria and Lebanon as a whole, the Sunni Muslims. In the nineteenth century, therefore, although Druze and Christians had fought bitterly among themselves between 1841 and 1860, they had been equally concerned with securing the maximum degree of autonomy from the Sunni Ottoman Empire; and as the Maronites and other Uniate Christians had looked for protection to France, so had the Druze looked to Britain. At the termination of the French mandate (1941-45), there were relatively few Lebanese Druze who preferred incorporation in a predominantly Sunni Syrian republic to remaining a minority in Lebanon.[5]

The Sunni community, on the other hand, had been enlarged by the creation of *Grand Liban* to become the largest

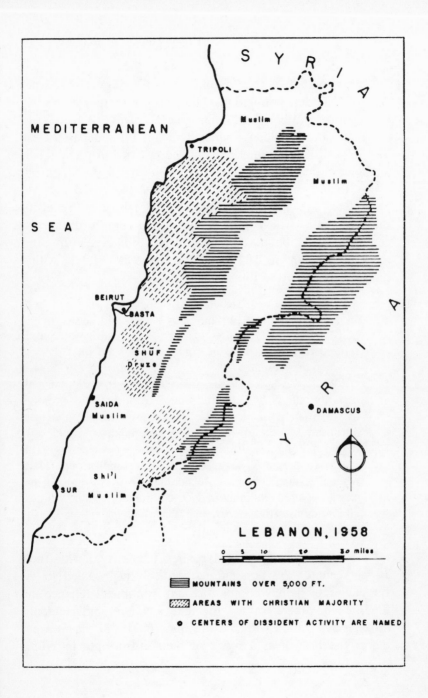

LEBANON, 1958

0 5 10   20 miles

▤ MOUNTAINS OVER 5,000 FT.

▨ AREAS WITH CHRISTIAN MAJORITY

⊙ CENTERS OF DISSIDENT ACTIVITY ARE NAMED

one next to that of the Maronites, numbering some 20 per cent of the total population. The strength of the Sunnis lay in the three traditional Ottoman coastal towns—Beirut, Tripoli, and Sidon (Saida)—which had not formed part of the Sanjaq, and in the hinterlands of the last two of these. Their leading political families thus felt loyalty not to Lebanon but rather to a "greater Syria" including Lebanon, and they regretted the loss to the Christians favored by the French of the ascendancy which they as Sunnis had enjoyed during the centuries of Ottoman domination. Accordingly, even after the establishment in 1926 of the Lebanese Republic within the framework of the French mandate:

> . . . the Sunnis were reluctant to share in the affairs of Lebanon. . . . While a few ambitious leaders did accept public office in spite of popular censure, the majority of Sunnis refused to take part in the running of a state the existence of which they resented.
>
> While the Sunnis refused to cooperate in Lebanese politics, the affairs of Lebanon tended to become the preserve of Christian politicians. The Shiites, who formed the least advanced section of the country's population, could only play a minor role; and the Druses, who were able and willing to cooperate, were a comparatively small group. Thus, while the Sunnis remained outside, the Christians took virtual charge of state affairs and added considerably to the political and administrative experience they had gained under the *mutasarriflik* [i.e., the Sanjaq].[6]

However, among the Maronites themselves, with their 30 per cent of the population, political rivalries led to divergencies of policy. Some favored continued reliance on the French; others wanted to make a bid for independence through association with the Muslims. By 1943, the weakening of the French as a result of their misfortunes in World

War II enabled Bishara al-Khuri, the leader of the second
faction, to reach an unwritten agreement with the Sunni leader
Riyad as-Sulh. In this so-called National Covenant (*al-Mithāq
al-Watani*), "Khuri, on behalf of the Christians, recognized
Lebanon as an Arab state that should never seek assistance
from any European power to the detriment of sister Arab
states. In return, Sulh vowed Muslim loyalty to Lebanon and
promised never to seek her dissolution in a larger Arab political unit."[7]

After shaking off the French mandate, independent Lebanon retained one peculiar institution that had come down
unchanged from the Sanjaq: the treatment of the religious
communities almost as the units of a federal state. Article 95
of the Constitution, as amended by the nationalists in November, 1943, read: "As a provisional measure and for the
sake of justice and concord, the communities shall be equi-
tably represented in public employment and in the composition of the Cabinet, such measure, however, not to cause
prejudice to the general welfare of the State." Thus, the
Maronite Bishara al-Khuri became President of the Republic,
the Sunni Riyad as-Sulh became Prime Minister, the President
of the Chamber of Deputies was usually a Shi'i, the Foreign
Minister an Orthodox Christian, the Minister of Defense a
Druze, and so on; and the Electoral Law, as successively revised, continued to prescribe, for the country as a whole
and for each electoral district, the religious sects from which
the parliamentary representatives should be proportionately
drawn.[8]

Riyad as-Sulh was so far loyal to the National Covenant
(and to the interests of his family) that he ordered the execution after a summary court-martial of the Orthodox Christian leader of al-Hizb al-Qawmi, who had attempted an
insurrection in 1949 to further the party's aim of uniting Leba-

non with Syria. In retaliation, Sulh was murdered by a party
assassin in 1951. Of the Sunni politicians who succeeded him,
none had his gift of leadership. Furthermore, though the
powers accorded to the President of the Republic by the Constitution were quite limited and ultimate authority was at-
tributed to the Chamber of Deputies as the representatives of
the people, the President had come to exercise, as if by force
of local habit, the autocratic authority of the former French
High Commissioner or the Ottoman Pasha. This finally led
to the overthrow of Bishara al-Khuri in the bloodless revolution of 1952 and the election to the Presidency of one of his
principal Maronite critics, Camille Chamoun (Sham'un). But
it was not long before Muslim leaders began to give expression
to a series of grievances (some of them well founded), charging that their communities were being discriminated against
by a predominantly Christian state apparatus.

The delicate balance on which the National Covenant de-
pended was thus already threatened in 1953. The expression
of these Muslim grievances in an English-language pamphlet
entitled *Moslem Lebanon Today* led to Christian protests and
a judicial prosecution which was countered some months later
by Muslim charges against an obscure young Christian writer,
who was duly convicted of a libel against the Prophet Mohammed.[9] The year 1954 had been designated by the Pope
as one of special honor to the Blessed Virgin,[10] and in Lebanon its celebration by the Maronites and other Catholics culminated in a well-publicized procession with a statue of the
Virgin from Beirut to her mountain shrine of Harisa. The
Muslims accordingly felt constrained to demonstrate their rival
strength and unity a month later by celebrating the birthday
of their Prophet with an exceptionally large torchlight procession in Beirut. But because of the organizers' lack of attention to safety details, this resulted in a fire and stampede in

which twenty-one persons died and several hundred were
injured,[11] not without some malicious satisfaction on the part
of some Lebanese Christians.

Nor was this the only factor in a rapidly evolving situation:

> The Egyptian *coup d'état* of 1952 and the rapid rise of
> Nasser captured the imagination of the Muslims of Lebanon,
> as it did that of Muslim Arabs everywhere. Lebanese Muslim
> opinion rallied around Nasser, and previously minor Sunni
> *maḥsūbiyya*[12] leaders stepped in to take advantage of the
> change. Thus Saeb Salam, who had previously been over-
> shadowed by Sami as-Sulh and Abdullah al-Yafi, rose to
> prominence as a Nasserist spokesman, with full support from
> Cairo and Damascus.[13]

Saeb Salam's father had been the leader of a Sunni opposition
to the French;[14] but as late as early 1956, his relations with
the British remained good. He was a director of Middle East
Airlines, a local company which became affiliated with British
Overseas Airways, and he was on a committee, presided over
by the British Ambassador, which was planning the establishment of a British-type public school in Lebanon as an attempt
to introduce character-building into a heterogeneous educational system (or lack of system) that seemed, as inspired by
the principles of Rousseau or John Dewey, to be deficient in
that very respect.

It is possible, however, that the enormous political success of Abdel Nasser's arms deal with the U.S.S.R. (in the
guise of Czechoslovakia) in September, 1955, convinced Saeb
Salam that the way to do international business was to "carry
a big stick." Lebanon's narrow width from east to west was
traversed by two oil pipelines, conveying a part of the product
of the Iraq Petroleum Company and of the Arabian-American
Oil Company to tanker ports on the Mediterranean at Tripoli

and Sidon, respectively. Each of the countries traversed by
these pipelines received a royalty calculated on the tonnage
of oil multiplied by the distance traversed, plus an additional
royalty for the provision of port facilities. Successive Lebanese
governments had, however, been dissatisfied for some years
that Lebanon should receive less than the other transit countries because of the exiguity of her territory; and the IPC's
negotiation in 1955 of a new scale of transit payments with
Syria (which the company was prepared to extend proportionately to Lebanon) was answered by a Lebanese demand
for complete parity of payment with the other transit countries.
The conduct of the subsequent negotiations was assumed in
1956 by Saeb Salam, who handled them with a stiffness to
which IPC was not prepared to capitulate, especially as it
now had a second pipeline operating to the Syrian Mediterranean tanker port of Baniyas which did not pass through
Lebanese territory. Salam's stiffness culminated, immediately
after Nasser's expropriation of the Suez Canal Company, in
a threat by him to nationalize IPC's Tripoli refinery.[15]

By the beginning of September, 1956, "the fierce spirit of
Muslim nationalism that [was] growing rapidly in the Arab
world" was reawakening the tension between Muslim and
Christian in Lebanon, and there was said to be reason to fear
that Salam's supporters in the Muslim quarters of Beirut would
cause disturbances if his intransigent policy were not followed.[16] The Anglo-French military action against Egypt at
the end of October (the Suez crisis) presented the Lebanese
Government with a dilemma for which President Chamoun's
previous policy of offering himself as a mediator in the frequent inter-Arab quarrels (e.g., the Egyptian denunciation of
the Iraqi Government for joining the Baghdad Pact) provided no guidance. Pressed by Egypt, the two Sunni members
of the Cabinet (Salam and the Premier, Abdullah al-Yafi)

wished to break off diplomatic relations with the British and
French "aggressors" and line up solidly with the other Arab
states;[17] but the rest of the Cabinet had regard for the thousands of Lebanese (mainly Christians) settled in French or
British dependencies. After a long debate, the two Sunnis
tried to force the government's hand by presenting their resignation.[18] The President accepted it, and found a Sunni elder
statesman (Sami as-Sulh, a survivor of the Ottoman tradition
of politics) ready to form an alternative Cabinet, with Dr.
Charles Malik as Foreign Minister.

Malik, for many years Ambassador in Washington and
Delegate to the United Nations, was well known for his pro-
Western inclinations, and his very inclusion in the new Government was a declaration of policy; but the Government
made its stand even more clear when it accepted the Eisenhower Doctrine in March, 1957.

During the months that followed the Suez crisis Lebanon's relations with Egypt and Syria became steadily worse.
Lebanon was never forgiven for having maintained diplomatic relations with Britain and France, and her acceptance
of the Eisenhower Doctrine made her the target of constant
attacks. When, in April, 1957, Lebanon allowed the Sixth
Fleet to stand by in Beirut while King Husain carried out
his *coup d'état* in Jordan, Cairo and Damascus branded the
act as treason, and Lebanon was furthermore accused of
being a hotbed of plots against the Syrian regime. All this
time the Sunni opposition in Lebanon was denouncing the
"treasonable" behavior of the Government and keeping in
constant touch with the Egyptian and Syrian authorities.
To the Sunnites, the acceptance of the Eisenhower Doctrine
was a distinct breach of the National Covenant, and implied
that the Christians were calling upon the United States to
replace France as their traditional protector and to intervene
in Lebanon on their behalf.[19]

Once out of office, Yafi and Salam set to work on forming a united opposition front. Parliamentary elections were
due to be held in June-July, 1957, and the personal grudges
of several Christian, Shiite and Druze leaders against
Chamoun[20] could be capitalized to embarrass the President's
supporters during the elections. Chamoun's term of office
was due to end in September, 1958, and the Parliament to
be elected was to select his successor; and it was already
feared that Chamoun might use a predominantly loyal Parliament to secure a second term of office.[21] The Opposition
demanded a neutral Government to supervise the forthcoming elections. When their demand was rejected they
staged a demonstration (May 30, 1957) in defiance of a
Government ban. The security forces disbanded the demonstration by force, and among those wounded was Saeb
Salam. It was not difficult to attract strong Maronite leaders
who cherished hopes of the Presidency . . . to the Opposition
camp. The Maronite partisans of Bishara al-Khuri, like the
patriarch, were already hostile to Chamoun. Yafi and Salam
had little trouble in winning over the Janbalati Druze. Kamal
Janbalat had helped Chamoun to office in 1952, but the latter
had not allowed him a free hand in the government, as he
had expected. He had, therefore, been opposing Chamoun
vigorously since 1953; and, although he did not disapprove
of the President's foreign policy and had no particular liking
for Nasser, he promptly joined[22] Yafi, Salam, and their Christian allies in what came to be known as the National Front
[the first Lebanese political front to be Muslim-led]. . . .
When Chamoun's supporters . . . won the elections by a vast
majority, many unsuccessful candidates, some of them unim-
portant, joined the National Front in illogical protest.[23]

Already, at the time of the formation of the Sulh-
Malik Government, there had been dynamite-throwing against
British and French buildings in Beirut, allegedly organized by
the Egyptian Military Attaché.[24] In February, 1957, a Syrian

colonel who had been sentenced to death *in absentia* for alleged conspiracy against the Syrian leftist regime was shot dead in a Beirut street. Other dynamite attacks on United States and Jordanian buildings in Beirut occurred after King Husain's counterrevolution in Jordan, and there was circumstantial evidence of arms smuggling over the border from Syria, organized (it was alleged) by Colonel Serraj's military intelligence in Damascus. The steady deterioration in security as the year drew to a close led the Lebanese Government to decide on swifter justice and sharper penalties for terrorism.[25]

Early in October, a self-styled "Third Force" consisting of Christian and Druze personalities had issued a manifesto in which they declared that one of the principal causes of the critical situation in which the country was

> . . . placed lies in the uncertainty about the renewal of the President's term of office. Such a renewal would be an attack on the inviolable character of the Constitution and would be directed against the very objectives that its drafters had in mind. Those Lebanese in responsible positions, to whichever faction they belong, do not seem aware of the consequences of their actions. Distracted from their proper duties, they are just adding to the uneasiness of public opinion and endangering public order. We see them defying the law and lowering the prestige of authority, while no coherent action is undertaken to deal with economic and social problems. They are thus the best agents of the Communism and the subversion which they claim to be fighting.[26]

On December 30, a delegation from this group called on President Chamoun and invited him to repudiate any idea of his seeking re-election. The President replied that while he had not changed his mind on the unsuitability of altering the Constitution, he would be obliged to "reconsider his position if he were not certain of finding a successor who would carry on his policy," an answer which naturally did not satisfy his interlocutors.[27]

The situation was made more acute by the proclamation on February 1, 1958, of the United Arab Republic (Egypt and Syria). The Lebanese opposition leaders Yafi and Salam and others flocked to Damascus to tender their congratulations and were told by the retiring Syrian President that Lebanon might join the union whenever she wished, retaining her own existence and culture;[28] a clash occurred on the northeastern frontier when Lebanese officials turned back thirty carloads of Lebanese Muslims, decked with Syrian, Egyptian, and pan-Arab flags, bound for the Syrian capital. Their enthusiasm for the new "union" was a clear challenge to the Lebanese National Covenant, and on March 4, the Maronite Patriarch gave the following equivocal reply to a Maronite sponsor of the Third Force who had asked him to clarify his position:

> We do not deny that the internal situation is causing us anxiety: corruption in the public service, an atmosphere of uncertainty, a stiffening on unreasonable principles, polemics that take the form of personal attacks, discord between the religious communities. We are concerned about the personal ambition of some among us who admit no limitation upon their aims. We are concerned about unbridled materialism. . . .
>
> From the bottom of our heart we invite all Lebanese of whatever party or community . . . to renew their faith in an independent, sovereign, and free Lebanon and work together in the spirit and the framework of their Covenant.
>
> We love our Arab brethren as we do ourselves. . . . We hope for complete success for every union and every agreement that they conclude among themselves.
>
> We have absolute faith in Lebanon, her independence, sovereignty, and freedom. We are convinced that collabora-

tion between Lebanon and the West, based on equality and mutual respect, is to the advantage of Lebanon on the economic and social as on the cultural level; we see in such collaboration every advantage for the Arabs. It is in such collaboration that Lebanon can serve the Arabs and safeguard their rights. Such collaboration is more useful than any action that might lead to a breach of relations between Lebanon and the West. . . .

To our Arab brethren everywhere we say that for the good of Lebanon and of the Arabs the independence of Lebanon must be maintained and strengthened. . . . We shall not join any union or federation, and we shall not accept anything that could weaken the sovereignty and independence of Lebanon.[29]

On March 28, there were riots in the southern town of Tyre (Sur) and sympathetic strikes in other towns of this predominantly Muslim region when five youths were sent to jail for trampling on the Lebanese flag and replacing it with that of the U.A.R.; the Minister of Education stated that a local college largely staffed by Egyptian teachers had had a good deal to do with the incidents. Two weeks later, there were disorders in the predominantly Druze district of the Shuf, revolving around the Druze aristocrat and opposition leader Kamal Janbalat, whose profession of socialism and attachment to the nonviolence of the late Mahatma Gandhi stood in marked contrast to the warlike enthusiasm of his feudal Druze henchmen. On April 19, the Maronite Patriarch spoke out again in a press interview against the "destructive egoism of those in high places in the present regime," and this time declared:

Everyone knows that the Arabs have for many centuries had a fair dream of unity. Providence has now given them honest and brave leaders, especially Gamal Abdel Nasser, who do not shrink from any sacrifice to hasten the revival of this part of the world. No wonder therefore that the Arabs turn with hope to President Gamal Abdel Nasser and his colleagues who symbolize their deepest aspirations. Personally, I am convinced that President Gamal Abdel Nasser desires for sovereign and independent Lebanon the same prosperity and well-being as for the Arab countries over whose future he presides. He asks only that Lebanon should not become a hotbed of plots against the Arab countries.[30]

Without replying directly to this, President Chamoun on the following day concluded a strong indictment of his critics, "the very persons who are directly or indirectly responsible for the attacks on public order and security," with these words: "The struggle for the Arab cause is a duty and an act of faith. I never thought that it could one day become, for some in Lebanon, a source of income, a springboard for attaining cheap popularity, and a stage for dwarfs and mountebanks." The Muslim religious leaders boycotted the official receptions marking the end of Ramadan, and the opposition replied to the President by charging him with financial malpractices: "Who shuttled to and fro between Baghdad, Cairo, Riyad, and Damascus to obtain airline concessions for certain companies? . . . One day we will tell the whole truth, and then the law will have its word to say." And spokesmen for the Third Force attacked the President's past record and impugned his desire to obtain, before the Chamber adjourned, a constitutional amendment which would enable him to be a candidate for the presidency when his present term expired in September.[31]

In this increasingly tense situation, on the night of May 7-8, Nasib Matni, editor of the opposition newspaper *at-Tilighraf,* was shot dead in Beirut.

Who killed him? A "loyalist"? But *at-Tilighraf*'s attacks on the President had not been among the most violent. One of the notables whom Matni used to attack without moderation or scruple in his paper? Very possibly. For this reason the editor had been wounded in an attack some time before. People have also said, *Cherchez la femme*. Whatever the truth of the matter, the cause of the murder has little historical importance; it was only a pretext, an indifferent pretext.[32]

The murder of Matni came at a very opportune moment for the National Front. A strike in protest, if sufficiently prolonged, could keep Parliament from meeting to consider the amendment of the Constitution. Opposition leaders also hoped that, faced with terror, riots, and street-fighting, Chamoun would resign and leave the country within three or four days. They were well subsidized by Egypt and Syria to carry on with the terror-imposed strike; and, since the Suez crisis, Syrian arms had been smuggled into Lebanon and distributed among their followers.[33]

On the day following the murder, the opposition called for a general strike, which their henchmen at Tripoli enforced on reluctant Christian shopkeepers. Supporters of al-Hizb al-Qawmi—former opponents of Lebanese independence, but now supporting the Lebanese Government against their bitter enemies of the Ba'th—resisted with force, and sixteen deaths were officially reported in three days. On the evening of May 11, frontier guards at Masna'a, on the main road from Damascus, searched the car of the Belgian Consul-General in Damascus (a fervent admirer of Abdel Nasser whose frequent crossings of the frontier in a heavily laden car had aroused suspicion) and discovered a considerable quantity of automatic rifles, pistols, and ammunition. On the next night, the post was attacked by 200 armed men from the Syrian side, who castrated and disemboweled five Christians manning the post and carried off the sixth, a Muslim, with them.[34] During these same days, disorders broke out in the Muslim quarters of Beirut, which the insurgents barricaded off against the authorities, and in the Shuf the pacifist Janbalat mobilized his Druze henchmen to attack the Presidential summer palace at Bait ud-Din but was opposed by the rival Druze faction, the Yazbakis led by the Minister of Defense, the conservative Amir Majid Arslan.

On May 11, the U.S. Ambassador to Lebanon, Robert W. McClintock, called on the Lebanese Foreign Minister, the Commander-in-Chief, and the President, in that order. He found Dr. Malik "in a considerable state of agitation. Malik claimed that Syria . . . had the night before dispatched a 'horde' of soldiers across the frontier to aid the rebels. Malik urgently requested that the Sixth Fleet be ordered to stand by ready to land in case the Lebanese government troops were overwhelmed." The Commander-in-Chief, General Fuad Chehab (Shihab), a member of Lebanon's most aristocratic family, was relaxing at his home fifteen miles from Beirut and "apparently taking a much less serious view of the situation . . . . anxious to keep himself and his Muslim and Christian subordinates[35] aloof from internal political troubles. He assured the ambassador that the current trouble was nothing to worry about. However . . . it might be wise for the United States Government to speed up deliveries of certain weapons it had promised the Lebanese Army." President Chamoun's attitude:

> . . . had changed markedly since dinner the evening before.
> . . . He charged that Nasser was making a "massive" attempt to overthrow him and replace him with a man less tied to America and more friendly to Egypt. The United States . . . must either promise to support him or else watch his and

every other pro-Western regime in the Middle East, including
Iraq and Jordan, fall like ninepins to the Egyptian.

Back at his Embassy office the Ambassador quickly dic-
tated telegrams reporting these views to Washington. To the
reports he added his own comment that, while Malik and
Chamoun's alarm was not fully justified, America's prestige
in the Lebanon was deeply involved and that the State Department should be prepared either to support the current
regime in resisting subversion or to cut its losses and learn
to live with a great Arab nation presided over by Nasser.[36]

While the guerrilla warfare in Lebanon continued inde-
cisively amidst a population still attracted by the pleasures of
feuding,[37] and the opposition continued to demand the President's immediate resignation as its condition for a cease-fire,
Dr. Charles Malik appealed to the U.N. Security Council to
pay attention to the threat to peace represented by the U.A.R.
intervention in Lebanon. The Egyptian spokesman denied any
such intervention, declaring that the revolution was a purely
internal Lebanese matter. The Council decided on June 11,
with the Soviet delegate abstaining, to send a group of observers (UNOGIL) to investigate whether men and arms were
being infiltrated across Lebanon's borders. During the following week, fifty-four neutral observers arrived in the country,
and on June 19 the U.N. Secretary-General himself arrived in
Beirut at the beginning of a tour of mediation among the
Arab capitals. On his return to New York, he stated at a news
conference: "The phrase you sometimes find used in the
newspapers, 'mass infiltration,' has not been and is not war-
ranted at present. I am sorry, I would correct myself on one
point. I would delete the words 'has not been' and say just
straight that to my knowledge we have no foundation for such
a judgment now."[38] This equivocal statement was immediately

seized on by U.A.R. propagandists as giving them a complete acquittal on the charge of intervention in Lebanon; but Lebanese Government newspapers were not alone in:

> . . . raising sharp questions about UNOGIL's adequacy even as an observer force when, for instance, it does not operate at night and its members have no command of Arabic. United Nations sources here point out, however, that although the observers are not running night patrols, they do stand 24-hour watches at their seven field bases, and they begin patrols at dawn each day.
>
> They also expect their four new reconnaissance aircraft to assist greatly in their coverage of the frontier—only 18 miles of which is still in Government control. Meanwhile, they are trying to recruit Arabic translators, possibly from local scholastic circles and from abroad, and they are cultivating cooperative relationships with most of the rebel leaders, especially in the frontier areas. . . .
>
> There is good reason to believe that Mr. Hammarskjöld and his assistants have embarked on a deliberate plan of trying to freeze the situation as it is at present until July 24, when it becomes possible to elect a new President. The belief is that this will give both sides time to cool off and encourage them to find a face-saving way out by eventually agreeing on a candidate.[39]

There is little doubt that this was also the desire of the U.S. Government, which had been sharply questioned concerning Mr. Dulles' statement on May 20 that the independence and integrity of Lebanon came within the Eisenhower Doctrine's interpretation of what was vital to the security of the United States. On July 1, Mr. Dulles said: "The presence of foreign troops, however justifiable—and it is thoroughly justifiable from a legal and international law standpoint—is not as good a solution as for the Lebanese to find a solution

themselves. It would be . . . a sort of measure of last resort."[40]
There seems to have been something of a contest of wills
between President Chamoun and the U.S. Ambassador in
Beirut, each insisting that the responsibility for inviting the
intervention of the U.S. Sixth Fleet lay with the other. The
Ambassador, who "held strong personal views . . . not all of
them in accord with Washington policies," had been pressing
"perhaps a little too enthusiastically for a compromise solution
of the conflict,"[41] while Chamoun and Malik were perhaps
too inclined to identify the independence and integrity of
Lebanon with their personal retention of power.[42] However,
the dispatch quoted above from *The Times*[43] ended with the
admission that the "sensible" notion of finding a compromise
candidate for the presidency had received no encouragement
yet from either side in Lebanon:

> The opposition leader, Saeb Salam,[44] has just declared
> that he will not recognize the validity of any election as long
> as President Chamoun is still in power; and since President
> Chamoun has repeatedly expressed his determination to con-
> tinue in office to the end of his term in September, the
> chances are that Lebanon may still spend the rest of this
> summer in a state of stubborn and costly anarchy.[45]

The powerful spring of the U.S. Sixth Fleet was, however,
being wound up to meet the possibility of a sudden emergency,
and it was triggered off by the Iraqi military *coup d'état* of
July 14.[46] While violent dispute raged for some weeks in the
U.S. and elsewhere about the propriety of the intervention
(followed by a British intervention in Jordan),[47] the success
of the Iraqi revolution came undoubtedly as an enormous
encouragement to the radical opposition in both Lebanon and
Jordan and a corresponding discouragement to the supporters
of those two hard-pressed governments who had been appeal-

ing for Western help; so that, except on the very dubious
hypothesis that it was in the Western interest to have the
whole of Syria, Jordan, and Lebanon (encircling Israel)
dominated by an Abdel Nasser still enthusiastically flirting
with the U.S.S.R., there was everything to be said for prompt
action. The Russians blustered, as at the time of Suez; but
those Western judges proved right who averred that the Krem-
lin was not ready to make the Middle Eastern issue a *casus
belli nuclearis* if the West showed a united front.

The landing of the U.S. Marines on the beaches just south
of Beirut precipitated an *opera bouffe* situation. The Lebanese
Commander-in-Chief, General Chehab, had "dallied and pro-
crastinated" since the beginning of the fighting, "refusing to
come to grips with the rebels"—partly because his army was
riddled by the same factions as were dividing the country, but
also probably because he was widely regarded as the compromise candidate for the presidency who might restore internal peace. On the morning of July 16, Chehab informed the
U.S. Ambassador "in no uncertain terms" that if the commander of the American Marines carried out his orders to
advance into the city, "Lebanese tanks, already deployed
along the airport road, would open fire"; on the other hand,
President Chamoun declared "equally emphatically" that if
they did not advance, he expected to be kidnaped by the rebels
issuing from their Beirut stronghold (the Basta quarter),
"leaving the United States in the embarrassing situation of
maintaining troops in a foreign country to protect a government which did not exist." The Ambassador devised a "truly
desperate expedient" of suggesting that General Chehab and
himself should "inject themselves personally between the opposing troops"; and this they did, accompanied by the Ambassador's poodle, finding "a dozen or more Lebanese tanks,
recoilless rifles, and other weapons lining the road, their guns

unlimbered and aimed directly at the spot where the Marine column was waiting." As a further face-saver for the Lebanese Army, the U.S. admiral in command agreed to divide the column into segments and place Lebanese jeeps in the intervals, "so that it doesn't look quite so much like an invading army"; and after an hour's delay ("General Chehab was clearly having difficulty persuading his staff to call off the resistance"), the cortege advanced, led by the ambassadorial Cadillac containing the Ambassador, the Lebanese Commander-in-Chief, the U.S. admiral, the Embassy *kavas,* and the poodle who on passing the embassy building was relieved by "a pretty embassy secretary."[48]

The next two weeks were spent in an attempt to obtain agreement on a compromise candidate for the presidency and a quorum for the Chamber of Deputies that would elect him. The government, which had issued warrants of arrest against several of the militant opposition deputies, announced a stay of execution for the period of the election. Saeb Salam continued to declare the present Chamber unfit to hold the election because it had been elected under government pressure the year before and now existed "under the menace of foreign troops"; but on July 31, fifty-six of the sixty-six deputies presented themselves, and on the second ballot General Fuad Chehab received forty-eight of their votes and was declared elected. The president-elect, whose term of office would not begin until September 24, prepared to negotiate a truce, but by August 8 there was a renewal of terrorism, probably arising from the failure to reach a compromise on the composition of a new Cabinet. The summoning of the U.N. General Assembly to examine the Middle Eastern situation, in an extraordinary session beginning on August 12, gave the opposition further occasion for resorting to violence in protest against having Lebanon represented in the Assembly by Charles Malik. Then,

on August 20, the representatives of the Arab states at the
U.N., who had been meeting in secret conclave, surprised
the world and perhaps themselves by solemnly confirming,
in the best spirit of Tartuffe, their adherence to Article 8 of
the Arab League Pact: "Each member state shall respect the
systems of government established in the other member states
and regard them as exclusive concerns of those states. Each
shall pledge to abstain from any action calculated to change
established systems of government."

As Chamoun's term of office entered its last days, there
was much talk of a new Cabinet to be headed by Rashīd
Karāma, who had been Premier once before and was now
titular leader of the revolt in his native city of Tripoli; but this
initiative was strongly opposed by the Katā'ib Lubnānīya
(Phalanges Libanaises), an organization made up mainly of
Maronites who had been among the most effective militants
on the government's side (given the abstention of the army,
to which the outgoing Prime Minister made bitter reference on
his arrival in voluntary exile in Turkey).[49] On September 22,
the Katā'ib called its own general strike, representing the
so-called "Christian counterrevolution," which was so far effective that the U.S. Ambassador felt constrained to mediate
between the Katā'ib leader, Pierre Jumaiyil, and the Prime
Minister-designate, who had meanwhile formed a Cabinet of
opposition personalities drawn from the various religious
communities. After "weeks of patient mediation, hopping in a
helicopter,"[50] the Ambassador succeeded in bringing the two
men together on October 10. Karāma tendered his Cabinet's
resignation and announced the formation of a new one on
October 14, consisting of two Muslims and two Christians
only; Jumaiyil himself, hitherto regarded as too extreme to be
acceptable as a minister on the compromise basis of the
National Covenant,[51] now became Deputy Prime Minister.

The strike was called off on the following day, the last of the
United States forces re-embarked during the next ten days, and
Lebanon could begin her slow and painful convalescence.
Some 3,000 people were stated to have been killed in the
months of fighting, *nearly one-third of them Syrians,* and
material damage had been heavy;[52] but the commercial aptitude of the Lebanese brought about a remarkably quick
economic recovery, and in the summer of 1960 it was possible
to elect a new Chamber of Deputies with only the customary
amount of brawling.

CHAPTER 8

IRAQ REVERTS TO TYPE

The causes of the Iraqi revolution of 1958 are not hard to find. The valley of the Euphrates and Tigris did not emerge from World War I as a long-standing political entity, but had latterly been administered by the Ottoman Empire as three provinces based on its three main cities; and under that administration, it had "passed from the nineteenth century little less wild and ignorant, as unfitted for self-government and not less corrupt, than it had entered the sixteenth."[1] As in Lebanon, there was numerically no majority community. Arabic was the predominant language, with important minorities speaking Kurdish, Turkish, and Syriac; but the Arabic-speaking population was divided nearly equally into Shi'is in lower Iraq and a somewhat smaller Sunni Arab community mainly to the north of Baghdad.[2] There were Jewish communities of long standing in Baghdad and Basra which played an important part in the commerce of those cities. Outside the cities, the social organization was predominantly tribal, and even the agricultural areas were populated (except for the Syriac Christian villages north of Mosul) largely by tribesmen who had only recently and reluctantly become sedentary and been reduced to tillage from the more "noble" (considered so

because it was less physically demanding) occupation of herd-
ing." "Surprising as it may seem, in view of the immense
antiquity of agriculture in the land of the two rivers, modern
Iraq is virtually a new agricultural country. Perhaps as much
as three-quarters of the area at present cultivated has been
brought under the plough since 1918, and one-third of it
since 1945. In Turkish times very little land was cultivated,
and the population was very small."[4]

It was this unpromising human and ecological material
which the British had undertaken after World War I to weld
together into a self-governing state which would at the same
time secure the British Empire's interests in communications
and oil. In the absence of any native leader who would be
acceptable to all communities and regions, the British had
brought in as king Faisal ibn Husain, that son of the Sharif
of Mecca who had most distinguished himself in the Arab
revolt of 1916-18 and had then in 1920 been ejected from his
briefly held throne in Damascus by a combination of French
intransigence and provocative Arab irresponsibility. Under
British tutelage, Faisal had gradually acquired some of the
arts of government,[5] but the establishment of a constitution in
1924 had inevitably admitted to the political arena a limited
class of urban lawyer-politicians whose contacts with the
illiterate rural masses or the smaller but growing class of
urban workers was only tenuous. A British administrator with
fourteen years' experience was reported as writing in 1930:

> I do not suppose there is in the whole of history another
> example of a state with a representative government of a
> modern type in which the only people who count are two or
> three hundred at the most. It is in fact a close oligarchy, but
> without the administrative experience, the education and the
> tradition of public service, without which as far as I can
> remember no oligarchies have governed successfully.[6]

In 1920, the urban nationalists, impatient for independence but lacking the physical force for an effective challenge of the British military administration, had exploited the local discontents of the tribal sheikhs along the Euphrates southeast of Baghdad to accomplish their objective, in the so-called National Revolution;[7] and in the following years, the British, driven by considerations of cost as well as political expediency to make their influence in Iraq an indirect one, had sought to conciliate tribal sheikhs, as the strongest social force in the country, by bestowing material and political favors in return for good conduct. The sheikhs, eager to turn the agricultural progress under the new regime to their personal advantage, exploited their political influence to get the tribal lands (hitherto state domain on which the tribes were theoretically tenants-at-will, but actually virtually uncontrolled by the government) registered as their own freehold; and the status of their tribesmen was thus imperceptibly degraded to that of serfs or peons legally bound to the soil. Dr. Warriner wrote in 1957:

> The prestige of the sheikhs rests on their former function of leadership in a tribal society which owed the state no allegiance. The foundation of the new kingdom strengthened them, giving them legal ownership of land and representation in Parliament, while it has at the same time weakened them by removing the need for tribal wars and tribal rule, through the creation of a national army and a national administration. They thus secured a position of privilege in the state, without obligation to it.[8]

Once the control exercised by the British had been reduced by the Anglo-Iraqi Treaty of 1930, and that of King Faisal I removed by his death in 1933, the urban politicians had split into rival factions which, when in opposition, did not scruple

to incite to insurrection against the national government of
the day those same Euphrates tribes whom in 1920 they had
incited against the British "oppressor."[9] So much genuine
patriotism (as Arnold Wilson's anonymous observer had pre-
dicted in 1930)[10] was there in these self-seeking pettifoggers!
The army officers, who were called upon to suppress the tribal
revolts, finally became disgusted by these sordid practices and
ejected the politicians in favor of a military dictatorship
(1936-37); but the spirit of factionalism was rife among the
officers also, culminating in the murder of the overweening
dictator Bakr Sidqi, and there followed an uneasy maneuvering
of political and military factions which finally led in 1940-41
to a deep schism between those who saw some value in maintaining the British connection and those who, in this first great
crisis of the Middle Eastern campaign in World War II, op-
portunistically but ineffectually intrigued with Nazi Germany
in pursuit of what were supposed to be the "national" or pan-
Arab interests.[11]

Notable among those who had not broken faith with the
British were Nuri as-Sa'id, who had been advanced to minis-
terial rank by Faisal I, and the Regent Abdul Ilah, representing the Crown during the long minority of King Faisal II.[12]
It is fairer to represent these men as moderate Iraqi nationalists, not as the British puppets caricatured by their enemies;
but the breach between them and the Istiqlal (Independence)
Party, which had compromised itself with the Nazis and paid
the price of incompetence and defeat in 1941 with exile or
wartime internment, was never bridged. After World War II
was over, the Istiqlal was recklessly ready to make common
cause with the emerging Communists in order to undermine
the moderates and the British alliance;[13] and Nuri (whose
personality more and more stood out above the political
dwarfs who opposed him)[14] was consequently compelled to

rely increasingly for support on that most conservative (not to say reactionary) section of the population, the tribal sheikhs,[15] and to distort the constitutional machinery to combat the demagogic appeal of his no less unscrupulous opponents.

It was doubtless this necessity, of securing ultraconservative supporters (in the absence of others) for the essentially reasonable policies that the ultranationalists rejected, that estranged Nuri from the one moderate leftist group in Iraq, the National Democrats. This group was briefly represented in one of Nuri's cabinets (1946-47), but resigned because it could not agree on what constituted "free" elections in a semi-tribal society like that of Iraq; and in 1954, Nuri suppressed the party for its collaboration with the Communists and sent its leader, Kamil Chadirchi, "a landowner of deep reformist conviction who . . . enjoyed the regard of much of the educated public,"[16] to jail on a charge of sedition. Nuri's education at the Ottoman military college from 1904 to 1906 had not included any insight into economic and social questions, and subsequently his early involvement in international affairs under Faisal I had left him with little inclination for what he (and almost all the Arab nationalists of his generation) regarded as the mere "bread and butter" of politics. Lord Birdwood tactfully concedes that, in the view of many, Nuri's failure:

> . . . lay in the absorption of the Government with long-term planning at the expense of short-term results with a popular appeal. . . . If only Nuri could have made fuller use of his publicity resources, he could have had the public behind him. . . .
>
> To take a practical example; a system of good roads is an essential element in planning the ordered development and progress of a community enjoying an expanding economy.

More particularly it could serve to break down divisions between tribe and town. But if this was not to be explained
to people who demanded houses, it would perhaps have been
wiser to have built the houses and neglected the roads.[17]

But, as a review of Birdwood's book pointed out, the defect
lay deeper:

> Nuri helped to lay the foundations of the State of Iraq—
> yet he was given no praise by the nationalists. He presided
> over the formation of the Development Board [1950-53],
> and the allotment to it of the greater part of the oil revenues
> —yet he was never given credit for trying to raise the living
> standards of his people.[18] Was this just because he was unable
> to handle modern methods of publicity? Was it because he
> despised the ordinary people so much that he did not con-
> descend to explain himself to them? Or was it because, al-
> though he did the right things, he did not do them in the way
> that his people valued? Lord Birdwood asserts the first and
> implies, perhaps unintentionally, the second. But surely the
> third is at least as important.[19]

Basically, the defect was that the capital investment was
undertaken in a country "in which the archaic social and
mental structures had hardly been changed at all. The development plan was thought of too much in terms of bricks and
mortar, and insufficient account was taken of the 'human
capital' that had to be improved and made more receptive
toward economic progress. Neglect of this was one of the
deep-seated causes of the indifference shown to the development plan, which undoubtedly contributed largely to the
downfall of the regime."[20]

The combination of indifference to the good aspects of
the development plans with frustration at their shortcomings
was strongest in that cross-section of the semieducated who
had no part in the immediate material profits to be derived

from the plans—namely, "the lower and lower-middle grades
of the administration and services, the junior teachers, the
part-time lawyers and newspaper editors, and all the under-
employed whom the educational system has created."[21] If
Nuri had been willing to be an intransigent nationalist of the
Syrian pattern and play the demagogue with this element, he
might at least have ended his days in dignified impotence, like
ex-President Shukri al-Kuwatly (designated the first Arab citizen of the United Arab Republic) or ex-Premier Mustafa an-
Nahhas; but as it was, the semieducated and maladjusted
products of Iraq's unequal growth during forty years of tutelage and self-government readily absorbed the malicious envy
which the Egyptian and Syrian regimes felt for Iraq's growing
oil wealth and consequent influence, as well as their refusal
to comprehend Nuri's appreciation of the geopolitical implications of Iraq's situation (with her northern border less than
150 miles from the Soviet frontier). For the pan-Arabs, Nuri's
unforgivable crime was not his social blindness, but his
reliance on the British connection. Less than two years before
Abdel Nasser made his fateful arms deal with the U.S.S.R.,
he had turned his formidable propaganda machine on Nuri
early in 1954 because Nuri had concluded a much smaller
arms deal with the United States; and this was only a fore-
taste of the vituperation loosed upon Nuri for concluding the
pact with Turkey which formed the nucleus of the Baghdad
Pact. Henceforth, no abuse was too violent, no lies too out-
rageous for the Egyptian propaganda mills, assisted by German experts who had served their apprenticeships with Dr.
Joseph Goebbels.[22] (The Germans found the Egyptians—
already adept in the native school of Abdullah Nadīm, Mustafa
Kamil, and the Wafd—ready pupils in the techniques of advanced mendacity.) From 1954 onward, those of Nuri's Iraqi
critics who slipped abroad to avoid his ban found a ready

welcome in Syria and Egypt; and it is safe to say that more of
the so-called Communists whose activities made Iraq a Western
journalists' byword in 1959 had received their indoctrination
in Damascus from the fellow-traveling Ba'th Party in the previous years than behind the iron curtain. Abdel Nasser himself
said in Damascus in March, 1959: "When Nuri as-Sa'id ex-
pelled them [the 'Communists'] from their country, we gave
them shelter. When Nuri as-Sa'id denied them everything in
their country, Damascus took them in and fed them."[23]

The collapse of Nuri's regime from the impact of the military *coup* of July, 1958 (the plans for which seem, significantly, to have originated after the Suez crisis),[24] was taken
by many observers as an unqualified triumph for Abdel Nasser
and his United Arab Republic; and one of the radical critics
of British policy in the Middle East could confidently declare:
"Only folly could suppose that natural development, free from
non-Arab influence of every kind, would lead anywhere but
to the unity at least of Egypt and the whole of Arabic-speaking
Asia, that is, not only the U.A.R. and Iraq, but also Jordan,
Saudi Arabia, the Arabian sheikhdoms and, ultimately, Aden,
with Lebanon in looser association."[25] But an obstacle was
soon to arise, apparently from the characteristically Arab
factor of personal *hubris*. The plot which had been hatched
for the overthrow of Nuri's regime was that a brigade commanded by Colonel Abdel Salam Arif should first attempt to
seize the strategic points in Baghdad and, if this failed, another
brigade commanded by Brigadier Abdul Karim Qasim should
repeat the attempt. The *coup* succeeded at the first stroke;[26]
and Arif's rapid promotion to the second highest position in
the new regime was evidently too much for his sense of dis-
cretion. It seems that his "impulsive, passionate, vain, and
indiscreet" temperament soon offended many of the other
officers who had been parties to the revolutionary plot, and

that they succeeded in convincing Qasim that Arif was a
liability to the regime. He had apparently conflicted at an
early stage with the left-wing elements among the officers,[27]
and the intemperate haste with which he extolled Arab unity
and the merits of Abdel Nasser gave rise to unrest among the
Kurdish minority and in the Shi'i cities that had no wish to
see their influence diminished by the merging of Iraq with
the predominantly Sunni U.A.R.[28] Arif was therefore successively relieved of his duties as Deputy Commander-in-Chief,
Deputy Prime Minister, and Minister of the Interior, and on
September 30 was appointed Ambassador to West Germany.
He refused to go, however, and apparently drew a revolver in
Qasim's presence; after a superficial reconciliation, he was
induced to leave for Germany on October 12. Following a
brief stay in Bonn, he went traveling in other European capitals and on November 4 returned without authorization to
Baghdad, where he was promptly arrested and charged with
conspiring to overthrow Qasim.

What the objective facts were that lay behind the charges
preferred against him in the People's Court (presided over by
Qasim's cousin Colonel Fadil Abbas al-Mahdawi, "a natural
buffoon who appears to delight in exhibiting the soul of a
dwarf"),[29] it is at present impossible to be sure. But one
commentator has remarked that while Arif had been making
his pan-Arab speeches during August and the first half of September, with the consequent reaction in the Shi'i south and
among the Kurds:

> . . . it appeared . . . that the Communists prepared to use
> these two movements for their own ends in the secret hope
> of taking control of them. The Iraqi Communist Party in
> fact took an extremely firm stand against any approach of
> Iraq to the U.A.R.; in this way it gained increasing support
> from the Kurds and those Shi'i circles most attached to Islam.

The extreme left thus acquired a formidable hold over the Baghdad government, to the extent that it could, if need be, threaten it with agitation or even serious disorders in the north and south of the country. To sum up, the attempts to strengthen Egyptian influence played into the hands of the Iraqi Communists.[30]

Arif's downfall had been accompanied by the arrest of a number of Ba'thi army officers and of Rashid Ali al-Gilani, the Istiqlal leader in the 1941 *coup* who had just returned from his seventeen years' exile. They were accused of plotting a pro-Egyptian *coup* with Arif, and the portraits of the Egyptian leader, with which the streets had been plastered immediately after the revolution, suddenly disappeared and were replaced with portraits of Qasim, the "one and only leader" (*az-za'īm al-awhad*).

> People in Baghdad began to speak cryptically of "Egyptian imperialism." When the Egyptian Minister of Education . . . visited the capital at the end of October, violent anti-Egyptian demonstrations broke out in the streets and at the University. Abdel Nasser's name was reviled, and his few Ba'thi supporters beaten up. The Egyptian rector appointed to preside over Baghdad University immediately after the revolution was asked to leave, and with him a number of teachers and technicians who had been invited to Iraq by two pro-Egyptian ministers in July and August. . . .
>
> In the view of Iraqi opinion the extreme left thus very rapidly emerged as the surest bulwark of the country's independence against the Egyptian designs upon it. To Cairo's dictatorial and centralized idea of Arab unity the Iraqi Communists very cleverly opposed a "liberal" and federal one. This idea of Arab unity, being more democratic and more "native,"[31] was calculated to attract the Iraqi intellectuals of the left who were offended by Abdel Nasser's dictatorial rule, and also the nationalist elements who prized Iraq's independence.[32]

Two important motives in this desire for independence of Egypt were the suspicion that Iraq's large oil revenues were coveted by capital-hungry Egypt and the Iraqi officers' scorn for the military prowess of the Egyptian Army as demonstrated in the Palestine War and the Sinai campaign of 1956.[33]

Abdel Nasser himself was said to have disapproved of the intemperate haste which Arif had shown;[34] but there seems little doubt that the Ba'thi and pan-Arab circles that were implicated in Arif's downfall had been superficial and unrealistic in their underestimation of the opposing tendencies in Iraq. As one of their spokesmen later admitted: "It cannot be denied that the inexperience, hastiness and operational clumsiness of the Arab nationalists in Iraq were as evident as the shrewdness shown by Iraqi Communist leadership. . . . The Arab nationalist movement had been gravely debilitated and its leadership paralyzed for so long under the Hashemites that when the old regime collapsed the vacuum could hardly be filled by the inexperienced nationalist leadership."[35] Once again, however, an Arab spokesman could not frankly admit an error without resorting to excuses that were unconvincing. If the nationalist "leadership" was so inexperienced, would it not have been more prudent not to break so utterly with the conservative nationalists like Nuri, rather than plunge the country into an uncharted sea of radicalism with Communist "shrewdness" for an ally? As for the "paralyzing" of the leadership by the "old regime," Nuri had directed his repression more against Communists than against nationalists. If the former were better organized to go underground than the latter, that was just an indication that Communism had more vitality than Arab nationalism;[36] and the failure of the nationalists to see beyond the immediate move in the political game was likewise a demonstration that they should have been content with a pastime like backgammon instead of essaying the complexities of chess.

CHAPTER 9

ABDEL NASSER AT DAMASCUS—
OR THE NEW SAINT PAUL

And immediately there fell from his eyes as it had been scales
(Acts of the Apostles, ix. 18).

At the time of the Iraqi revolution in 1958 and the subsequent landing of U.S. troops in Lebanon and British troops
in Jordan, Abdel Nasser had been visiting Marshal Tito in
Yugoslavia. He flew immediately to Moscow and conferred
there on July 17-18 with the Soviet leaders. During the
debates in the extraordinary session of the U.N. General
Assembly, harmony between the delegates of the U.A.R. and
the U.S.S.R., in opposition to the American and British "aggressors," seemed complete. In October, Nasser's faithful
acolyte, Defense Minister and Commander-in-Chief Abdul
Hākim Āmir, visited Moscow and concluded an agreement
there by which the U.S.S.R. would finance the Egyptian High
Dam to the extent of 400 million rubles and provide technical
assistance. About the same time, the Ministry of Education
ordered that Russian should be taught in place of French in
Egyptian schools, and an Egyptian correspondent reported
that in a year's time there would be 2,000 students from the

U.A.R. studying in Communist China, instead of the twenty-two there at present.[1]

However, in a speech in mid-November, Abdel Nasser indicated that these friendly relations with the Communist countries existed "despite the difference of our social systems":

> When I visited the Soviet Union and met their friendly people I declared in the name of the U.A.R. that we are a people that is friendly to those who behave as friends, and that struggles against those who are hostile. . . . We are a people that remembers kindnesses. . . . They have their social order, we have ours. . . . Arabism is a socialist, democratic, cooperative society uniting the sons of this land.[2]

This element of unity was emphasized in a reorganization of the central government of the U.A.R. announced on October 7. It set up under Abdel Nasser a central government of twenty-one members, of whom fourteen were Egyptian and seven Syrian. Of the Syrian Ba'th leaders, Akram Hawrani and Salah ud-Din Bitar were called to Cairo as Ministers of Justice and National Orientation respectively; and though Colonel Serraj remained in Syria, it was as Minister of the Interior in the northern province, subordinated to a trusted Egyptian Minister of the Interior (Zakariya Muhi ud-Din) in the central government. This was considered a strengthening of Egyptian control over a Syria that might now (the first rapture of the U.A.R. honeymoon being over) be tempted to draw closer to a republican Iraq.[3] In August, a former organ of the outlawed Syrian Muslim Brotherhood had been suspended for stating that a Syrian-Iraqi union was more natural than one between Syria and Egypt, and Syrian students had been forbidden to study in iron curtain countries because of the "disloyal" attitude of the Syrian Communist Party toward the U.A.R.[4]

On November 27, consistent with his statement two weeks

earlier about the friendly relations existing with the Soviet
bloc, Abdel Nasser declared that "the imperialists are now
trying to sow discord between the U.A.R. and the Iraqi Republic and between their respective leaders. But in vain will
they try to provoke differences; between Cairo and Baghdad
there is full collaboration in confronting imperialism and
Zionism."[5] On December 7, however, the Beirut Sunni politician Saeb Salam, who was in Cairo apparently to give an
account of his stewardship during the Lebanese civil war,[6]
told a reporter after a long interview with Nasser that "Communism in Iraq was the greatest danger threatening the Arab
world" and blamed the United States for serving the Soviet
Communist turn by not siding with the U.A.R. against Qasim's
"separatist" policy.[7] On December 8, the Baghdad radio announced the discovery of another alleged plot, this time apparently by the nationalist Istiqlal, though the government-
controlled Middle East News Agency of Cairo accused the
U.S. of being behind the plot.[8] By mid-December, a U.A.R.
official could tell a reporter that "unless Britain and America
change their policy in Iraq quickly, there is no hope of saving
that country from Communism"; the Cairo weekly *Akhbar
al-Yawm* for the first time informed the Egyptian public directly that Iraqi Communists were hostile to Arab nationalism
and accused them of attacking Arab unity and the U.A.R.;
and in response to the return to Syria of the Communist leader
Khalid Bakdash and his public criticism of the U.A.R., the
Damascus radio for the first time attacked Communist tactics.[9]

The stage was now set for Abdel Nasser to reveal himself,
which he promptly did in a speech delivered at Port Said on
December 23 to celebrate the "victory" of 1956:

> When the people of Egypt united with the people of
> Syria, when the standard of Arab nationalism again streamed
> victorious, then enemies lined up against us. They felt that

the victory of Arab nationalism and the standard of Arab
nationalism would ruin all their interests, whether they looked
toward exploitation or opportunism. . . .

Reactionaries knew that Arab nationalism would forbid
exploitation; the Communist Party knew that Arab nationalism would destroy opportunism; so reactionaries and the
Communist Party declared themselves against Arab nationalism and Arab union. . . .

During these last days, since the creation of the U.A.R.,
I have proclaimed that the nation must constitute a National
Union.[10] We must unite our efforts so as to destroy Zionism
and crush imperialism. We shall not be able to struggle
against Zionism or against imperialism if we are struggling
against ourselves. But the Syrian Communist Party has refused that. . . . Still more, it has rejected Arab nationalism
and Arab union. Some of its members last week preached in
favor of separation and rejected any union of the Arab
nation. That is what Zionism preaches.

He went on to admit that there had been some delays in
reorganizing the economy and administration of the "Syrian
province" after its incorporation in the U.A.R. and said that
he had now appointed a commission of three (Akram Hawrani
and two of Nasser's Egyptian Army colleagues) "to accelerate
the rhythm of modernization."[11] The attack on the Syrian
Communists was echoed two days later in an interview which
his Syrian acolyte Serraj gave to the Egyptian newspaper
al-Ahram:

At the beginning the opportunist elements—the Communists—were carried along by the current of Arab nationalism and accepted the union, but against their will. For a time
they watched and waited; but having realized that their hopes
were vain and that the union was going its course step by
step, they became the resounding spokesmen of reaction and
opportunism. . . .

Recently the Communist Party has openly shown its hand. Its leaders in their statements have urged secession, by a hidden and vile means. They have spoken, not of union, but of federation, a utopian idea.[12]

The day before Nasser made his speech, commented the Lebanese businessman and politician Emile Bustani, "many people had been of the opinion that Arab nationalism and Communism were synonymous," but now "local nationalists echoed his words and rounded up their local Communists"[13] to the number of several hundred in Syria. This led Khrushchev, at the Twenty-first Communist Party Congress of the U.S.S.R., to extend a warning to "certain leaders of the United Arab Republic" that "to struggle against Communist parties and other progressive parties is the work of reaction"; and this was followed by an attack by the Syrian Communist leader Khalid Bakdash (who had again slipped away behind the iron curtain) upon "those adventurers, the leaders of the Ba'th Party, who have lost all prestige in the eyes of the people. They are trying to use the slogan of the struggle against Communism to incite the liberated Arab country to abandon the policy of positive neutralism, to stifle democratic liberties, and finally to open the doors to imperialist capital investment from Western Germany, Italy, Japan or the International Bank dominated by American capital."[14] Nasser, however, was anxious not to forfeit the advantages of Soviet economic aid, notably the construction of the first stage of the High Dam and of a new shipyard at Alexandria for which agreements were now being signed with the U.S.S.R.; and in his speech on February 21, 1959, to celebrate the first anniversary of the establishment of the U.A.R., he was accordingly concerned with finding scapegoats:

Immediately after my speech at Port Said, plots were set afoot for the purpose of making trouble between us and the

U.S.S.R. Our relations with the U.S.S.R. have always been friendly, based on mutual respect and on the principle that each country would choose the political and social regime it wished and would collaborate with the other without interfering in its internal affairs. But naturally imperialist circles seized on the opportunity to sow discord. . . .

Foreign news bulletins directed at Russia said that the U.A.R. was turning toward the West, separating itself from the U.S.S.R., beginning to realize the Russian danger. . . . The news that reached Cairo said that Khrushchev had decided to get rid of Gamal Abdel Nasser because he was an obstacle in the way of his policy. News directed at other countries said that Russia had organized a plot to have Abdel Nasser murdered and that Yugoslavia[15] had drawn the attention of the U.A.R. to this plot. These were only lies and devices to sow discord. We had to pay attention to them because the imperialist powers and also the opportunists were trying to achieve the same end.

He went on to describe his recent exchange of letters with Khrushchev, and then discussed his relations with the Iraqi Government since the revolution of 1958:

We knew that the traditional imperialist policy had been at all times based on the creation of differences between Baghdad and Cairo. We knew that the enemies of nationalism would not fail to use these old methods again. A first attempt aimed at dividing the people into two clans, one calling for union with Egypt, the other asking for a federation. I then gave my frank opinion. I said that there were some points I could not discuss, union being one thing and federation another,[16] but that I was ready to discuss Iraq's relations with the U.A.R. We could arrive at a military and economic agreement, thus expressing the sense of union. If union was to be achieved, we would prefer it to be done unanimously. I also pointed out the danger for the Iraqi people of becoming divided between supporters of union and supporters of federation. I naturally felt that some of those who were advocating federation and attacking union did not have the situation in Iraq in mind at all, but Syria. They wanted to rouse the Syrian people against union.[17]

Two days later, he declared in Damascus, "We shall not allow opportunists to divide the U.A.R. and Iraq. We form a single people and the Iraqi people is part of the Arab nation."[18]

Already at the beginning of February, Qasim had re-formed the Iraqi Cabinet, excluding the remaining supporters of the U.A.R. and consequently strengthening the left;[19] and the People's Court had tried Colonel Arif and sentenced him to death.[20] From this time on, those pan-Arab Iraqis who had left the country to escape the new "persecution" began to plot a *coup d'état* with agents of the U.A.R.; the Mediterranean correspondent of *The Christian Science Monitor,* who in his Beirut headquarters was absorbing and reflecting these *émigrés'* sentiments, reported that "it is almost certain that Communist control of Iraq now could be overthrown only through armed action of some kind";[21] and it was significant that Abdel Nasser prolonged his stay in the Syrian province. The northern Iraqi city of Mosul, whose leading families were hostile to the proposed Iraqi land reform and, indeed, to control from Baghdad in general, was situated conveniently near the eastern frontier of the Syrian province. Arms were smuggled in with the complicity of an Iraqi brigade commander, Abdul Wahhab Shawwaf, and officers of the Syrian intelligence made contact with Iraqi officers. But Qasim had his informers at work and sent a large contingent of the Communist-directed Popular Resistance Forces (al-Muqāwama ash-Sha'bīya)[22] from Bagh-dad to reinforce a congress of the Partisans of Peace author-ized in Mosul from March 5 to 7. Clashes between them and the Mosul supporters of Abdel Nasser led Shawwaf on March

8 to come out openly against the Baghdad regime, which he
accused of having "thrown thousands of innocent citizens into
internment camps, the like of which had never been seen in
the past under the rule of the oppressor Nuri as-Sa'id and the
criminal Abdul Ilah."[23] The U.A.R. flag was run up the citadel,
and warriors of the Shammar tribe, whose lands on either
side of the Syrian-Iraqi frontier were exposed to the effects of
the land reform, approached the suburbs of the city. But
Qasim's air force bombed the rebels; the Popular Resistance
Forces and Kurdish irregulars sprang into action against the
apparently irresolute regular army garrisons; Shawwaf was
wounded by a bomb fragment and then, as he lay on a hospi-
tal bed, finished off by a noncommissioned officer with his
own revolver. The rebellion fizzled out, to be followed by a
terrible revenge on the part of the Popular Resistance Forces:
thirty to fifty officers were said to have been shot out of hand,
civilian suspects were hunted down and killed, and the Iraqi
air force took a pitiless toll of the fugitive Shammar as they
fled back to the Syrian frontier.[24]

Following the Mosul revolt and its failure, the floodgates
of Arab mutual vituperation were opened between the capitals
of the U.A.R. and Iraq, and the depths to which human nature
could sink in "envy, hatred, malice, and all uncharitableness"
were revealed. The Baghdad radio accused the U.A.R. of
having fomented the revolt, and Nasser replied from Damascus by accusing Qasim, "the divider of Iraq,"[25] of "using the
methods employed by Nuri as-Sa'id and the enemies of Arab
nationalism." A fugitive Iraqi officer who had died in Syria
of wounds received at Mosul was given a state funeral at
Damascus and buried near the tomb of the great Saladin,
whom the U.A.R. Government had from the start proclaimed
as its spiritual forerunner.[26] Placards carried in the funeral
procession read: "Qasim the traitor has sold his country to

the Communists"; "Death to Qasim and Mahdawi"; "Shaw-waf, you shall be avenged"; "Honor to Arif, hero of Arab nationalism." In return, the Baghdad radio described Abdel Nasser as:

> . . . a bloody dictator and dangerous charlatan who claims to be the champion of Arab nationalism; but we may ask if Arab nationalism is a synonym for conspiracy, murder, and shameless dictatorship. The Mosul rebels in Cairo's pay have massacred innocent civilians, men, women, and children, have sacked and plundered the city like highway robbers. To justify these massacres Abdel Nasser has found no better excuse than to accuse the Iraqi Government of Communism and atheism. In fact everyone knows that he wants to impose on the Iraqi people his dictatorship and his imperialism, whose ferocity is not to be compared even with that of the nineteenth-century Ottoman domination.

Nasser, still in Damascus, replied: "When we see what is happening in Baghdad seven months after the death of Nuri as-Sa'id, we realize that terrorism has reached a pitch that it had never known under Nuri's rule; we realize that the domination of an atheist and subservient minority is even more ferocious than in Nuri's time."[27] This exchange of verbal courtesies was accompanied by rival parades; in the one at Baghdad, a photograph of Nasser's head was mounted on various obscene model bodies, while at Cairo Nasser's acolyte, "Field-Marshal" Abdul Hākim Āmir, presided over a silent procession in which Qasim was represented as a cat hanging from a rope.[28]

On March 19, Khrushchev—who had already extended a mild reproof to Nasser three days earlier, to which the Egyptian leader had replied with insufficient deference—said to press correspondents: "The President of the U.A.R. has rather gone off the handle. He is still young for his position, he's impulsive. He wants to take upon himself more than he can carry." To this, Nasser replied at Damascus on November 22:

> It is not only Abdel Nasser who is young and impulsive, but the whole Arab people that is enthusiastic and impulsive. Without this enthusiasm and ardor we should not have been able to achieve the great miracles at a time when we counted only on God and ourselves. . . .
>
> On October 29, 1956, when Egypt was invaded, we rose to defend our country. From October 29 to November 6 [the day of the cease-fire], we stood alone facing Israel, Great Britain, and France. . . . During those days we saw no sign of help from any country whatsoever, including the Soviet Union.[29]

Less than two months earlier, however, Nasser's confidant, the editor of *al-Ahram*, while already talking back to Khrushchev, had spoken of "our thanks for the help which the Soviet Union gave us . . . in our struggle and fight for life and liberty,"[30] and earlier statements had been still more explicit with reference to the Suez crisis.

On April 17, Abdel Nasser gave an interview to the editor of the Indian left-wing magazine *Blitz,* who asked: "Haven't you been rather rough in resisting the [Communist] danger? After all, Qasim and the Communists are Arabs. Couldn't you be patient in the hope that they will recover their senses and understanding?" To this and the following questions, Nasser gave these very revealing answers:

> The Arab Communists have sold themselves to foreign influence and forfeited their standing as Arabs. They are tools in the hands of Russia, and that country's agents in Iraq, Syria, and all parts of the Arab world. That is why we cannot trust them as Arabs. Because of their behavior in Iraq and Syria we can wait no longer. I did all I could to con-

vince them, but they decided to turn against their fatherland.
It was therefore my duty to draw my fellow-citizens' attention
to this new danger and arouse them against this threat. As
for us Arab nationalists, we have no ally either in the Communist or in the imperialist camp. Similarly, the arms we
possess are neither those of the Communists nor of the imperialists. That is why I turned to my people. My people is
my army and my strength, and the armor of my faith. . . .

We have our own doctrine of Arab nationalism based on
Arab solidarity and on the idea that we form a single nation.
. . . Hence every Arab state has the right to defend the inde-
pendence and the Arab character of Iraq against Britain,
America, Russia, or any other great power.[31]

The refuge which Russia has given to Arab Communists
like Bakdash, and the front seats given them at Moscow,
Sofia, and elsewhere while their hostile attitude to their
fatherland was perfectly well known, seemed to us a flagrant
violation of international diplomatic etiquette. Suppose I did
the same with Bulganin, Shepilov, and Zhukov! . . .

The stand I took against the Iraqi Communists was an
Arab matter and had nothing to do with the Russians; but
Khrushchev . . . accused me of using the language of the
imperialists. . . . I had therefore no other course than to tell
the Russians that we did not like this new kind of imperialism. . . . Russia lost in less than three weeks all the good
repute she had gained among us in three years. . . .

All we ask is that people should not interfere in our
affairs. Khrushchev knows the harm that the Baghdad Pact
did in our part of the world by bringing into it the poisonous
atmosphere of the cold war. Why repeat the mistake the
West made at Baghdad? Is the group of Communists who
do not honor their fatherland more important in Khrushchev's eyes than the friendship of a great ocean of Arab
peoples extending from the Persian Gulf to the Atlantic? . . .

Until quite recently Khrushchev supported us. For every

move on his part in favor of the Arabs, we have been grateful
ten times over. But for every blow that he levels against us,
we will give him ten in return.

That is our policy. Perhaps you will say it is not a policy
of patience or wisdom. But we are proud of our honor. . . .
For all our lives we have struggled against imperialism. . . .
We know how to use the proper means to defend ourselves
against it. Now this new danger threatens us. . . . The battle
is just beginning. We sincerely hope not to have to fight this
battle on an international scale. The Communists and the
imperialists must understand that we are the masters in our
own country and that . . . neither Eisenhower nor Khrushchev has the right to behave in this way in our country.

The British are still suffering from their attack of "Suez
dizziness." They are like wounded wolves. They want to take
revenge on me because I snatched Suez out of their hands.
That is why, to destroy me, they are using every tool that
comes into their hands, from Qasim to the Communists.[32]

In Iraq, as the summer came on, Qasim evidently followed
a policy of temporization. His statement in May that the
country was not yet ready for a return to interparty rivalries
seemed a rebuff to Communist pressure for seats in the Cabinet, and the anti-Communist majority in the National Democratic Party deferred to the "one and only" leader's fiat by
voluntarily suspending its activities.[33] The death sentences
passed by Colonel Mahdawi's demagogic tribunal against such
survivors of Nuri's regime as the ex-Prime Minister Fadil
al-Jamali were still not executed, in spite of Communist demands; the unlimited power hitherto given to the Popular
Resistance Forces to arrest and search was withdrawn, and
they were brought under stricter military control; and the
Chief of Staff and Military Governor of Baghdad, General
Ahmad Salih al-'Abdi, became increasingly prominent as a
non-Communist upholder of the army's authority. Faction-

alism, however, remained endemic in the country and seemed not so much a consequence of the new-fangled ideologies of Communism and nationalism as a retrogression to the historic Arab factionalism (Yemen and Qays, Hinnawi and Ghifari, etc.) in village and, to some extent, urban society.[34] It now found expression in:

> . . . the strange political map which every Iraqi carries about in his head these days. This map divides all the sections of Baghdad, and all the provincial capitals, indeed all the villages of the country up into "Nationalist" and "Communist." . . . The striking feature of this map consists in its really having a concrete reality. To cross from the Communist-dominated Kadhimiye section of Baghdad to the Nationalist Adhami section means to cross an invisible border. Even the political slogans on the walls . . . change radically. The inhabitants of the two sections face each other with knives at the ready; they would certainly be at each other's throat were it not for the army standing between them.
>
> Out in the country the situation is quite the same: Kerbela is Nationalist, Nejef is Communist, Musaiyeb is Nationalist, Mahmudiye Communist. Every Iraqi can extend this list *ad libitum.* . . . This map dividing the country up into a chessboard pattern of red and black squares . . .[35]

At the celebration in July of the first anniversary of the revolution, serious rioting broke out in the oilfield center of Kirkuk, with its mixed population of Turkomans and Kurds:

> The Turkomans, who have lived in the old city since Ottoman times . . . represent the stable city-community; merchants and proprietors of all kinds are Turkomans. The Kurds . . . are more dispersed and on the average less prosperous. There had been trouble between the two communities ever since Colonel Shawwaf's revolt in March.
>
> Although it would be gross oversimplification to class all

the Kurds of Iraq as pro-Communist, a large section among
them have long considered Soviet aid essential to their goal
of an autonomous or independent Kurdistan. . . .

The Turkomans, however, proved resistant to Communism; in several trade unions, they outvoted their pro-
Communist Kurdish and Arab colleagues. Approving Kassem's
attempts to contain the Communists, the Turkomans prepared
to celebrate the anniversary of the revolution by erecting 133
triumphal arches at the expense of their community. . . .

Quarrels broke out between the Turkoman celebrators
and the Kurdish Communists. Fights at the city's bridge, in
the two cinemas, and in one of its biggest cafés, ended with
several persons wounded, and most of the Turkoman triumphal arches were burned. Then the Communist-dominated
People's Resistance Forces stormed the police station, looted
the arms stored there, and drove the Turkomans into their
homes.

Troops of the Second Division, composed largely of
Kurds, were sent to Kirkuk to restore order, but instead took
the side of the Kurds. Some of its units shelled Turkoman
houses and the troops were soon in command of the whole
town. . . .

On July 15 and 16, the Communists, with the help of
the Second Division, ruled in Kirkuk. Refugees coming in to
Baghdad reported that a red flag flew over the town and army
cars were roving the deserted streets, their loudspeakers
giving orders in the name of the National Front. A committee
consisting of the secretary of the local Communist party, the
mayor (a Communist), and six Kurdish officers, exercised
supreme power, and had designated the homes of anti-
Communists to be looted by the "mass organizations" and the
People's Resistance Forces. The mayor, according to the
refugees, had ordered the executions of several groups of
Turkoman notables and had them buried in mass graves outside the town.

The mutiny in Kirkuk was finally put down by 50 armored cars under Colonel Fuad Aref, the brother of the imprisoned Abdul Selim Aref [Abdel Salam Arif]. A few days later, Kassem gave out the number of dead as 120, the majority "executed" by the Communists in conditions of great cruelty. Kassem himself is said to have visited Kirkuk on July 21 or 22. On his return, he showed the press photographs taken there and blamed "a faction which I do not wish to name" for the atrocities. Furious, he claimed to have proof that the unnamable faction had planned risings all over the country.[36]

Faced with this official condemnation of the Kirkuk massacres, the Communist Party saw fit to publish a lengthy manifesto drawn up by its central committee at a meeting later in July. After deploring the refusal of the National Democrats to participate in the National Front, which had led to a series of "negative results," the Party proceeded to evade responsibility for recent excesses:

Recently the encroachments on citizens' rights and freedoms have grown worse, and some persons have consequently been driven to adopt a negative attitude toward the national authority. This negative attitude has prevented the government from seeing the real danger, which comes from imperialism, reaction, and the enemies of the republic. Faced by the continued provocations on the part of reactionaries who have shed the blood of citizens and violated their sacred rights, and faced by the hateful attitude of some reactionary elements who have escaped the purge of the state administration, the people (moved by the will to defend their existence, to preserve the advantages they have gained, and to safeguard the republic) have sometimes reacted violently. These reactions have sometimes led to abuses and ill-considered punitive measures. . . .

But the revolutionary drive of the Iraqi people is a positive thing which has always . . . played a very important part in bringing down the foundations of the former regime. . . . It has deep roots and beginnings going far back into the history of the Iraqi people. In the course of centuries, the people underwent the worst forms of oppression and enslavement at the hands of invaders and usurpers. That is why in many risings and revolutions the people have reacted very violently and often with much bloodshed. The popular masses have consequently preserved for many generations a spirit of vengeance against the reactionary forces. . . .

The lynchings perpetrated by certain politically backward popular masses, the tortures practiced on detained persons, the looting of property, the infringement of the rights and freedoms of innocent citizens, are methods deplored by all those engaged in the revolutionary struggle against the enemies of the republic. . . . But our Party, not having shared the responsibility of government for a single day, is the one which least of all, in these conditions of unrest and conspiracy against the country, is able to stop the tortures practiced on the internees.[37]

In its own suffocating jargon, the manifesto examined the reasons for certain mistakes of policy:

From the earliest days that followed the revolution, all applicants were admitted as members of the Party. . . . As a general rule, those who were enrolled as members *before* the revolution became, at various levels and degrees, the nucleus for expansion *after* the revolution. . . .

While our organizations have made important advances as far as their quantitative development is concerned, the Party managers have found that qualitatively the development has not followed a parallel course. . . . The contradiction between the Party's quantitative development (which has advanced) and its qualitative development (which has shown some shortcomings) has increased. The reason for this lies in the fact that all the organizations have had to apply themselves to different and numerous political tasks of major importance, which has prevented them from achieving a qualitative development parallel to or approximating its numerical advance.

This situation has had negative aspects, since the capacity of the organizations to grasp and remain faithful to the Party's ideology and policy has declined, consequently impairing the guiding role which they should have secured in the mass movement, to cope with the spontaneous pressures from below. Thus some comrades have behaved as individuals—putting themselves on the same level as the masses that belong to no party and thus lack adequate understanding —instead of giving directions and guidance to these masses.[38]

Finally, the report criticized both an excess of "bureaucratic centralism" in the Party and the existence of certain "deviations":

> Titoist revisionism has not been entirely unsuccessful in finding support in the Arab countries. The opportunists who call themselves Arab Communists dream of splitting the Communist movement in our country and all the Arab countries. However, they have not succeeded and will not succeed in undermining the unity of our Party.[39] . . .
>
> The opportunist elements have tried in vain to form a hostile faction. In spite of their setback, the opportunists and revisionists will nevertheless go on with their maneuvers. They will doubtless find individuals, among those who have been expelled from the Party and other suspect elements, who will lend a willing ear to their claptrap. . . .
>
> Mistaken behavior and acts are the reflection of mistaken concepts and ideologies. Insofar as we may commit errors, mistaken concepts contrary to Marxism-Leninism are born in our minds, the product of vanity and of the dizziness that

comes from success. Groups belonging to the petty bourgeoisie are at the root of these concepts. . . .

In present circumstances the process of re-education aims above all at eliminating mistaken leftist concepts. . . . Some comrades who have a leftist mentality see the situation not as it is but as their imagination presents it. Their plans and concepts are therefore not based on a correct estimate of the real forces at work, but on an overestimate of our strength and an underestimate of the part played by the nationalist bourgeoisie in the national struggle. . . .

Furthermore, the general political struggle calls for caution so as not to make mistakes on the right in reaction to the leftist mistakes. It is a mistake to hold the Party responsible for measures taken against the democratic movement, and to overlook the role of the nationalist bourgeoisie marked by its uncertain wavering to and fro. . . . Important sections of the bourgeoisie have at present antidemocratic concepts which they themselves fought against under the former regime. . . .

We must play our part in educating the non-Party masses. We must strongly oppose mistaken slogans and excesses, and once and for all give up the idea that "to oppose excesses weakens the revolutionary spirit of the people." The indifference we have shown in the past toward the commission of excesses should be a lesson to us. The Party must take disciplinary measures against those who are shown to have violated the Party's principles and taken part in these excesses.

At the same time we must firmly resist all ideas and behavior that spread a feeling of defeatism and surrender among the masses or weaken their confidence in their own strength, the strength of the Party and of the national movement, for safeguarding the republic and guaranteeing the rights of the people.[40]

For the time being, it was clear that the drive toward Arab-world revolution under Abdel Nasser's leadership had stopped short of its objective; and in the middle of 1959, he turned, not unlike Stalin some thirty years earlier, to an alternative of socialism in one country—his United Arab Republic—with a new slogan promising to double the standard of living in ten years.[41] This change was accompanied by a marked surface improvement in relations between the U.A.R. and the U.S., which was probably prompted by the disclosure that the former's holdings of foreign exchange had been depleted by one-quarter during the year ending on September 1;[42] by a month-long tiff between the U.A.R. and Communist China over an official reception given in Peking for the Syrian Communist leader Bakdash; and by the withdrawal of U.A.R. students from the Soviet-bloc countries that led to premature self-congratulation that "the honeymoon between the Communist bloc and the Middle East is over."[43] American propagandists for the U.A.R. were soon in full cry;[44] and when the Ba'th made an abortive attempt in October to murder the Iraqi dictator, "liberal" correspondents were positively ghoulish in their anticipation (based on assurances from those pan-Arab *émigrés* whose third failure in twelve months this was) that the next time the plot might be more successful.[45] The U.A.R. acknowledged having received U.S. surplus farm products in the value of $107 million over the past year; and in December, the International Bank made a grant of $56.5 million for the deepening of the "nationalized" Suez Canal (work which the former "imperialist" Company had planned to finance out of revenue),[46] despite the U.A.R.'s continued seizure of cargoes purchased from Israel, in disregard of a compromise formula devised as recently as July by the U.N. Secretary General.[47]

While West German, Italian, Japanese, Austrian, British, and American entrepreneurs were said to be touting round the Egyptian dictator with offers of loans, he asserted his "positive neutralism" by encouraging the nationalists of Cuba

and Panama in their anti-U.S. campaigns and by allowing
Egyptian "civilian patriots" to found a museum at Port Said
to commemorate the suffocation of a British lieutenant (over-
powered by six Egyptians) during the fighting in 1956[48]—
this last as an immediate offset to the reluctant re-establish-
ment by the U.A.R. of diplomatic relations with the United
Kingdom and Australia. At the ceremonial starting of work
on the Aswan High Dam in January, 1960, Abdel Nasser
boasted of "the victory of the Arab nation" over the "forces
of tyranny, occupation, enslavement, and domination,"[49] and
the Moscow radio reported that he had awarded Khrushchev
a gold medal to commemorate the U.S.S.R.'s exclusive role
in the first stage of the dam; but simultaneously, the U.A.R.'s
Minister of Culture was inviting other nations to provide
$100 million to prevent the ancient Egyptian monuments
upstream from the grandiose new "monument" from being
submerged by its waters. The Mediterranean correspondent
of *The Christian Science Monitor* printed a dispatch (January
14, 1960) entitled, with characteristic optimism, "Political
Maturity Grows in Mideast"; but in February, the U.A.R.
was trying to resurrect the phantom Arab Palestine "state"[50]
and consequently renewed its attacks on the Jordan Government for its unwillingness to relinquish the territory on the
west bank of the River Jordan for what was, in effect, the
cause of U.A.R. self-aggrandizement. In March, Abdel Nasser,
returned from a month's much-needed reorganization of the
government of the northern province (i.e., Syria), called for
thousands of volunteers to go to fight the French in Algeria.

The Arab boycott against Israel had proceeded from an
embargo on her goods and shipping, through an embargo on
third-party shipping carrying goods to or from Israel, and
thence to a blacklisting of foreign firms trading with Israel
and of ships and their crews that had called at Israeli ports.[51]

After the U.N. Secretary General admitted on April 8, 1960, that his efforts to bring about a mitigation of the second of these practices had thus far failed, Finnish and Swedish seamen's unions announced their refusal to handle cargoes from ships flying the U.A.R. flag; and on April 13, an Egyptian ship (the *Cleopatra*) in New York was picketed by American seamen and longshoremen; the president of the Seafarers' International Union complained that a month earlier the crews of three vessels under contract to his union had been "abused, maltreated, and held virtual prisoners" in Egyptian ports.[52] A week later, the Swedish counter-boycott was called off, and the U.S. State Department declared that while it did not condone the Arab boycott, the New York counter-boycott was embarrassing the conduct of U.S. foreign relations. Amid reports from Cairo that Abdel Nasser had narrowly escaped poisoning by an Israeli agent recently,[53] the executive committee of the International Confederation of Arab Trades Unions (notoriously a creation of U.A.R. pan-Arab policy,[54] now meeting in Cairo) gave the U.S. a seven days' ultimatum to end the New York counter-boycott or face a counter-counter-boycott of U.S. shipping in all Arab ports. Nasser stated in a television interview broadcast in the U.S. on April 26 that Arab workers regarded the New York counter-boycott as "an action against their country and affecting our dignity"; and on the following day, the chairman of the U.S. Senate Foreign Relations Committee, Senator Fulbright, accused "special pressure groups" of trying to push U.S. policy "in special-interest directions." While President Eisenhower, in a press conference on April 27, disclaimed knowledge of "any idea whatsoever of making a new step" toward securing free passage for all nations through the Suez Canal (thus belying his confident assurance three years earlier),[55] Congress overrode the protestations of Senator Fulbright and others and wrote into the foreign-aid program an amendment inviting the President to withhold foreign aid from any nation waging economic warfare against any other nation benefiting from the program.

On April 30, the Arab counter-counter-boycott "from the Arabian Gulf to the Atlantic Ocean" began to take effect, and among the first U.S. ships affected were some carrying wheat and flour to Arab countries, to be paid for in their local "soft" currencies, which payment would then be returned to the Arab governments as a loan; the transfer of these relief cargoes to third-party ships would be at Arab expense and might imperil the continuation of this form of U.S. aid. On May 6, however, this crescendo of folly was ended by a compromise whereby the New York counter-boycott was lifted in return for a State Department undertaking "to renew its effort to assure freedom of the seas and to protect the interests of our shipping and seamen now being discriminated against by the Arab boycott and blacklisting policy." On May 8, the day before the Arab counter-counter-boycott was lifted, Abdel Nasser proclaimed an Arab victory; coupled the U.S. with Britain, France, and Israel; expressed "thanks and appreciation to the Soviet Union for her wise and noble policy toward us"; and gave his assurance that "the strong friendship binding the peoples of the U.A.R. and the Soviet Union will never be affected by political and social differences."[56] Apparently, the *bakhshish* of more than $150 million which the U.S. had dispensed to the Egyptian dictator during the past year and a half had, despite Senator Fulbright's effort to retrieve it now by a hasty visit to Cairo, been washed under the *Cleopatra's* stern. Coming to the U.N. General Assembly in September as the U.A.R.'s "neutralist negotiator for peace," Abdel Nasser on his arrival in New York paid the conventional verbal tributes to the United States; but less than a month earlier, on

August 29, 1960, his government-controlled organ, *al-Gumhuriya,* had declared: "Russia has supplied us with a loan of 900 million rubles for the High Dam, while America has supplied us with 900,000 refugees from Palestine. . . . Russia gave us experts and officials, and America spies and intriguers." While ancient Egypt had been ruled under the "double crown," revolutionary modern Egypt, and now the U.A.R., was kept going by a systematic practice of double-talk.[57]

CONCLUSION

As Cardinal Newman wrote more than a century ago, "I am not a politician; I am proposing no measures, but exposing a fallacy and resisting a pretense."[1] This fallacy and this pretense are that the problems of the Arab world today are primarily those of the economic development and social evolution of an "underdeveloped" region, and that they can be meaningfully understood without regard to the political cross-currents by which it is tossed. That this *is* a fallacy and a pretense has recently been noted by two writers on the economics of the region;[2] but in a more general application it seems to have escaped the notice of that distinguished liberal economist Professor John Kenneth Galbraith, when he emphasized the harm done to the United States in allowing foreign aid to "the less fortunate lands" (a new euphemism for "underdeveloped," which was itself a euphemism for "backward") to be misused by "corrupt tyrannies or reactionary ruling oligarchies."[3]

The condition of being an "underdeveloped" country is not merely an economic one. The deficiency is not usually confined to the economic sphere, but extends to the spheres of political experience and public responsibility as well. Hence, there is a fair degree of probability that "the less fortunate lands" will be subject to governments with an appreciable tinge of oligarchy or tyranny or both, of corruption or reac-

173

tion or both. Moreover, the infusion of foreign aid "without strings attached"—i.e., what in a simpler age was called "something for nothing"—has the almost automatic effect of *stimulating* corruption among the oligarchs; and when they are criticized by the "nearly-haves"—those who are kept just outside the charmed circle of privilege[4]—they naturally tend to respond (being oligarchs) by repressive and tyrannous behavior. This is what has happened not merely in the Arab world, but recently in Turkey; and though there was nothing strange about the Turkish *coup d'état* to those acquainted with the political facts of life in the Middle East, it came as a shock to those who had deluded themselves into thinking that the Turkish republic had been "made safe for democracy," had received its initiation through the Truman Doctrine and NATO into the "American way of life."

In fact, the principal lesson that Turkey's Prime Minister from 1950 onward, Adnan Menderes, had learned from the United States was how to make himself into a Turkish Huey Long. Marshall Plan aid was relatively successful ten years ago precisely because it was given to European governments that already had a substantially developed sense of public responsibility and needed only to be helped financially and technically over the disasters of World War II. But where governments are deficient in public responsibility, the over-trusting application of foreign aid may merely *breed* irresponsibility; and responsibility is conspicuously not multiplying as rapidly as the regimes that have asserted their "independence" during the present century: modern Turkey and Iran; Egypt, Iraq, and Syria; India, Burma, and Ceylon; Indonesia, Korea, and Vietnam; Jordan, Cyprus, and Somalia; Ghana and Guinea, Mali and the Congo . . .

> That it may please thee to give to all nations
> unity, peace, and concord;

We beseech thee to hear us, good Lord. . . .
That it may please thee to strengthen such as do stand;
    and to comfort and help the weak-hearted;
    and to raise up them that fall;
    and finally to beat down Satan under our feet;
We beseech thee to hear us, good Lord.[5]

THE EGYPTIAN LAND REFORM

The program of land reform undertaken by the Egyptian revolutionary regime from September, 1952, onward consisted of three initial reforms and two supplementary but essential developments:

1) The maximum permissible holding was fixed at 200 *faddān* (a *faddān* is approximately one acre), with an additional 50 *faddān* allowed for each of two sons of the landowner. The surplus was to be expropriated, with compensation payable in government bonds in the value of 70 times the annual tax assessment of the area expropriated. As successive governments favorable to the landowning interest had for two decades allowed the land tax to remain virtually constant while land values had been sharply rising, the state was thus at last recouping itself for this legalized fraud upon it. The land thus expropriated, as well as that seized from members of the "former royal family" without compensation, was to be allotted to landless peasant families in lots of three to five *faddān*, and each former estate or other appropriate unit would be under the direction of a cooperative committee which would include representatives of the Ministries of Agriculture and Social Affairs. It was admitted that the land thus available

177

for redistribution would not suffice for more than about 10 per cent of Egypt's millions of landless peasants.

2) The agricultural tenant, estimated at 38 per cent of the rural population, would be served by fixing the maximum annual rent of his plot of land at ten times the annual tax assessment, thus permitting the tenant (instead of the land-owner) to benefit from the previous artificially low level of the tax assessment.

3) The day laborer, particularly common in the over-populated provinces of upper Egypt, was to benefit from the fixing of a minimum wage.[1]

These reforms were good in principle, though a well-wisher of the new regime admitted that the motive behind them was as much political and psychological—the manifest breaking of the power of the landowners who had dominated the Wafd as well as the smaller parties—as economic and social.[2] Moreover, in 1958, complaints were voiced in the government newspaper *al-Gumhuriya* itself that the coopera-tives and rural welfare units attached to them were being run more for the benefit of the bureaucrats staffing them than for the *fellahin,* and that the laws designed to protect the tenant and the laborer were both being extensively evaded under pressure of the iron laws of supply and demand operating in this country of acute rural overpopulation.[3]

Since this condition made it evident that land reform in itself could not provide the means of raising the standard of living to any great extent, the new regime looked for means of increasing the crop area and providing power for new industrial purposes. These were the practical objectives of the celebrated High Dam, though once again the psychological profits to be derived from this surpassing of the Pyramids were not lost on this prestige-hungry regime. Almost as soon as the blueprints of the High Dam were ready, and long before the problem of financing the grandiose undertaking had been solved, the regime had embarked on the ambitious development of an area of the desert west of the Delta, the "Liberation Province" (*Mudīrīyat at-Tahrīr*), which was designed to be irrigated from the additional water provided by the High Dam. But Abdel Nasser's application to the Dam project of his policy of "positive neutralism"—i.e., playing off the U.S.S.R. and the West in the hope of extracting the maximum *bakhshish* from both—caused three years' delay (1955-58) in getting even a paper agreement on the financing of the first stage of the Dam; and meanwhile, the officer-bureaucrats entrusted with the Liberation Province had embarked on an expensive piece of "social engineering"[4] which degenerated into window-dressing and "boondoggling" until it was exposed and had its appropriations drastically reduced. In 1958, this experiment presented to a Western visitor as forlorn a spectacle as Mo-hammed Ali's premature experiments in the industrialization of Egypt a century earlier, prompting the reflection:

> What . . . is wrong with all this well-meant enthusiasm, with all this ambition to force the pace of "progress"? The Egyptian planners, we came to conclude, lack respect for organic growth. They fail to see their fellowmen, the *fellahin*, for . . . persons, with their own rights and dignity within the never-ending rhythm of life and death as manifested in this part of the world. In the name of progress these people are being torn out of the context of everything that has made their life and that of their ancestors in the past. "Your life is not worth living," it is being decided for them. They are moved and transplanted to the desert for a planned, better future, with the results we have seen. Reforms, yes; but obviously these ought to be introduced gradually, with the start being made at the roots: that is, with life as it is in the villages now existing.

The fact that the Liberation Province project shows a

clear tendency to collapse within itself and that nothing more promises to result from the huge expenditures and investments than a very small thrust into the heart of the desert certainly is regrettable as far as the waste of funds and energies is concerned. But is it not also somehow a cause for rejoicing? For it seems to show that the forces of down-to-earth life, of plain human common sense, of the laws of a free society, are stronger in Egypt after all than the wilfulness of the Government.[5]

By 1959, the realization that so much time had been lost over the preliminaries of the High Dam led Abdel Nasser's regime at last to a compromise with the Sudan Government on this issue; but the propaganda machine was meanwhile seeking to maintain optimism by other expedients. One of these was the "discovery" by a member of the Cairo University faculty of agriculture that "the greatest reclamation project of our century" could be undertaken by the systematic raising of subterranean water along the line of the Western Desert oases from Kharga to Baharīya, about 150 miles west of the Nile Valley. It was doubtless true that modern techniques could, at a price, increase the water supply for irrigation purposes there, and make possible a larger population than the existing 40,000; but it was claimed that the population in ancient times had been 8 million,[6] apparently a mistaken inference from a figure which conservatively estimated the population of ancient Egypt as a whole. A government propaganda publication went on to claim that this "New Valley reclamation project" would develop on a large scale the "experiments" undertaken in the Liberation Province. There, some 25,000 *faddān* had been brought under cultivation; but the New Valley project was "a gigantic 3 million *faddān* operation" (nearly 5,000 square miles) which "will help expand Egypt's cultivable land by 50 per cent."[7]

Early in 1960, Abdel Nasser's regime was negotiating with the West German Government for financing a canal to flood the Qattara depression (a natural obstacle that had hampered Rommel and his Afrika Korps in 1942) from the Mediterranean and utilize the fall of water for hydroelectric purposes. West German sources had likewise given financial and technical assistance in constructing the first steel furnace in the Middle East, located just south of Cairo at Hulwan (formerly Helouan-les-Bains), using (initially, at least) imported German coke, but intending eventually to use the Egyptian iron ore of the Aswan region.[8] In these and similar projects, there was doubtless some potential utility; but they had to be seen in the context of Abdel Nasser's extravagant declaration in 1959 that (notwithstanding the uncontrolled growth of Egypt's population by about a half-million every year) he would double the *per capita* national income in ten years, starting in 1959. Indeed, his government was claiming that in the eight years since the Revolution of 1952 they had already raised the living standard by 50 per cent; but according to a visiting American economist, most competent observers would not concede more than an increase of about 1.5 per cent per annum since 1955. The ordinary budget for 1960-61 and the development plan budget showed deficit financing to an extent of some $700-850 million, with a national income of $1.25 billion; and the writer of the article on "Egyptian Agrarian Reform" (previously cited) ended on a barely concealed note of menace: "During the next decade the Chinese example may well attract increasing attention, especially if western indifference to the basic problems of the underdeveloped nations [*sic*] continues. And time is running very short."[9]

NOTES

NOTES

INTRODUCTION

1. This is only gradually being understood by inhabitants of the United States, who have been taught that their forefathers made a revolution 200 years ago, though it was, in fact, primarily just a secession, a much milder and less radical operation; *see* Frederick Gentz and Stephen Possony, *Three Revolutions Compared* (Chicago: Henry Regnery Co., 1959).

2. John C. Campbell, *Defense of the Middle East* (New York: Harper & Brothers [cloth ed.], Frederick A. Praeger [paper ed.], 1960), p. 370.

Chapter 1

THE MYTH OF THE FOURTEENTH MUSLIM CENTURY

1. *Der Mythus des 20. Jahrhunderts, eine Wertung der seelischgeistigen Gestaltenkämpfe unserer Zeit* ("The Myth of the Twentieth Century, an Evaluation of Conflicting Mental and Spiritual Types in Our Time") (Munich: 1930).

2. *See* Albert R. Chandler, *Rosenberg's Nazi Myth* (Ithaca, N.Y.: Cornell University Press, 1945), p. 6: "The term 'myth' in this title does not mean something that is untrue, but something which is true in a profounder way than science or common sense. It means a view of life and nature that is accepted on faith and inspires social action. It is a kind of cult or religion or intuitive philosophy."

3. Philadelphia: J. B. Lippincott Co., 1939.

4. *Islam in Modern History* (Princeton, N.J.: Princeton University Press, 1957), p. 112.

5. *Ibid.,* pp. 49–50; italics added.

6. *See* Kirk, *The Middle East in the War, 1939-1945* (London and New York: Oxford University Press, 1952), pp. 56–78; I. S. O. Playfair, *The Mediterranean and the Middle East (History of the Second World War,* United Kingdom Military Series [London: Her Majesty's Stationery Office, 1954-56]), vol. II, chap. ix; Majid Khadduri: *Independent Iraq* (2nd ed.; London and New York: Oxford University Press, 1960), pp. 177 ff.

7. *See* Gideon Weigert, "Arab Writers Look at Israel," *The World Today,* no. 15 (1959).

8. *See* Kirk, *A Short History of the Middle East* (6th ed.; New York: Frederick A. Praeger, 1960), pp. 315–21.

9. *See ibid.,* pp. 309–14.

10. Nissim Rejwan, "Arab Nationalism in Search of an Ideology," in Walter Z. Laqueur (ed.), *The Middle East in Transition* (New York: Frederick A. Praeger, 1958), p. 148; he is citing Sa'adun Hammadi, of Wisconsin University.

11. Quoted in Sylvia G. Haim, "Islam and the Theory of Arab Nationalism," in Laqueur, *op. cit.,* pp. 280–81.

12. Quoted in Rejwan, *op. cit.,* p. 155.

13. Abd ur-Rahman Azzam, in Washington on May 5, 1960.

14. *See* Hazem Zaki Nuseibeh, *The Ideas of Arab Nationalism* (Ithaca, N.Y.: Cornell University Press, 1956), index (for page references).

15. *See* Leonard Binder, "Radical Reform Nationalism in Syria and Egypt," *The Muslim World,* no. 49 (1959).

16. *See* Rohan D'O. Butler, *The Roots of National Socialism* (London: Faber & Faber, 1941).

17. *See* Sir H. A. R. Gibb, "The Evolution of Government in Early Islam," *Studia Islamica,* no. 4 (1955), p. 17: "The nemesis of the over-rapid conquests of the Arabs—and the political tragedy of Islam—was that the Islamic ideology never found its proper and articulated expression in the political institutions of the Islamic states."

Chapter 2

THE SAPPING OF THE SEVEN PILLARS

1. Of contemporary journalists, Hal Lehrman was perhaps the only one percipient enough to explain the British motive; *see* the quotation in Kirk, *Middle East in the War,* p. 344 n. 5.

2. Nuqrashi's leader, Ahmad Mahir, a more robust personality who was perhaps better equipped to withstand the gusts of popular extremism, was murdered by Egyptian extremists a month before the establishment of the Arab League.

3. *See* Kirk, *Middle East in the War,* pp. 472–73, 482–83.

4. *See* Kirk, *The Middle East, 1945-1950* (London and New York: Oxford University Press, 1954), pp. 119–20; note the Egyptian reaction to the Labour Government's appointment of the consistently "soft-centered" Lord Stansgate to lead the British delegation negotiating a revision of the Anglo-Egyptian Treaty.

5. *See ibid.,* pp. 57–67; and Robert Rossow, Jr., "The Battle of Azerbaijan, 1946," *Middle East Journal,* no. 10 (1956).

6. For the reaction of one Zionist (and holder of a British passport) to this achievement, *see* Jon Kimche, *Seven Fallen Pillars* (1st ed.; London: Secker & Warburg, 1950). The title of the present chapter is adapted from his title.

7. For examples, *see* Viscount Montgomery, *Memoirs of Field-Marshal Montgomery* (London: William Collins Sons & Co., 1958; Cleveland, Ohio: The World Publishing Company, 1958), pp. 418–20, 422, 424–25.

8. The term "old oligarchs" is borrowed from Alfred E. Zimmern, *The Greek Commonwealth* (5th ed.; London and New York: Oxford University Press, 1931), p. 458.

9. *See* Pierre Rondot, *"Tendances particularistes et tendances unitaires en Syrie,"* *Orient,* no. 5 (1958), p. 143; he speaks of "the leaders of the first governments of independent Syria, dedicated to the national struggle but with little administrative experience, consumed by patriotic fervor but incapable of sustaining the effort against Zionism."

10. *See* Jon Kimche, "Iraq Breaks with Britain," *Nineteenth Century and After,* June, 1948.

11. *See* Gideon Tadmor, "The Syrian Scene," *Middle Eastern Affairs,* no. 3 (1952).

12. *See* below, chap. 5.

13. There are passages from Nagib's *Egypt's Destiny* (London: Victor Gollancz, 1955; New York: Doubleday & Company, 1955) that are worth quoting at length because they tell quite another story:

> In July, just before the second truce, my forces were badly defeated at the battle of Negba. Mawawi [Major-General Ahmad Ali al-Mawawi] had rejected my own plan of action in favour of one of his own, which was so faulty, in my opinion, that I refused to carry it out. He relieved me of my command but, as soon as he realized that we were going to be defeated, he asked me to command our withdrawal. . . .
>
> A few days later I appealed to Mawawi for reinforcements to make up for the heavy casualties that we had suffered. He refused to believe that our losses had been as great as I said they were and accused me of trying to blame him unjustly for our defeat. In front of several staff officers he berated me in terms that I could not accept, and so I demanded that he apologize. When he refused to do so I told him what I thought of him in terms as strong as those he had used in describing me. I then returned to my H.Q. and drew up a written report of what had happened. I submitted it to Mawawi with the request that he apologize in writing. Instead he ordered me to report to G.H.Q. in Cairo. . . .
>
> Back in Cairo I cursed myself for what I had allowed to happen. It was not the first time, nor the last, that I have had occasion to regret my violent temper. All I had achieved on this occasion was to place the entire responsibility for the war in Palestine on the inadequate shoulders of Mawawi [pp. 22–23].

Later, Nagib describes how, when he was about to mount an attack, one of his brigadiers "made a bitter remark . . . 'May God send you a bullet if you get us into any more trouble than we're in already' " [pp. 26–27]. Those familiar with the Middle East will recognize the leitmotiv, the attempt to shift responsibility on to someone else.

14. *See* Gamal Abdel Nasser, *The Philosophy of the Revolution* (Buffalo, N.Y.: Economica Books, 1959), p. 29. Nasser confirms the fact that, during the Egyptian-Israeli armistice negotiations at the beginning of 1949, he discussed with an Israeli officer "Israel's struggle against the English, how [they] organized [their] underground resistance in Palestine and how [they] succeeded in mobilizing world public opinion" against the British.

In the early weeks of the Palestine War, while the Egyptian Army was already engaged in Palestine, the Egyptian Government rejected a British proposal for a political compromise in the Anglo-Egyptian Sudan (Kirk, *Middle East, 1945-50,* pp. 140–41).

15. *See* Kirk, "Egypt: The Wafd and Great Britain, 1950-1," in Peter Calvocoressi and Konstanze Isepp, *Survey of International Affairs, 1951* (London and New York: Oxford University Press, 1954), p. 261; and cf. Anthony Eden, *Memoirs: Full Circle* (London: Cassell & Co., 1960; Boston: Houghton Mifflin Co., 1960), pp. 236–37 (Br. ed.), pp. 262–64 (U.S. ed.).

16. Jean and Simonne Lacouture, *Egypt in Transition* (London: Methuen & Co., 1958; New York: Criterion Books, 1958), p. 143.

17. *Ibid.,* pp. 140–41.

18. *Revolt on the Nile* (London: Allan Wingate Publishers, 1957; New York: The John Day Co., 1957), pp. 103–4. Anwar as-Sadat's account of his collusion with the Nazis in 1941-42 makes interesting reading (pp. 36–51). Generals Wavell and Auchinleck would have trembled to know what a formidable opponent was working against them; but in the end "Egyptian treason prevented the revolution from taking place. . . . England, unlike Carthage, was not to be destroyed" [pp. 50–51].

Chapter 3

THE FREE OFFICERS LOSE THEIR FREEDOM

1. *See* Walter Z. Laqueur, *Communism and Nationalism in the Middle East* (London: Routledge & Kegan Paul, 1956; New York: Frederick A. Praeger, 1956), pp. 59–60.

2. *See* Eden, *op. cit.,* pp. 233 and 237–38 (Br. ed.), pp. 255 and 263–64 (U.S. ed.).

3. Lacouture, *op. cit.,* p. 213; and Kennet Love, in *The New York Times,* November 21, 1954.

4. Eden, *op. cit.,* pp. 256–57 (Br. ed.), pp. 284–85 (U.S. ed.).

5. Eden, *op. cit.,* pp. 254 and 260 (Br. ed.), pp. 282 and 289 (U.S. ed.). For a discussion of the internal contradictions in the social structure of the Wafd Party, *see* Francis Bertier, *"Les forces sociales à l'oeuvre dans le nationalisme égyptien,"* *Orient,* no. 5 (1958), pp. 77–82.

6. *See* below, Appendix.

7. *See* Kirk, *Middle East, 1945-1950,* pp. 129 and 132–34; and Calvocoressi and Isepp, *op. cit.,* pp. 267–68. The first Egyptian statesman to establish contact with the Sudanese Independence Party had been Nagib al-Hilali when he was Prime Minister, three months before the revolution (Calvocoressi and Isepp, *Survey of International Affairs, 1952* [London and New York: Oxford University Press, 1955], pp. 206–7).

8. Revolutionary Council communiqué to the foreign press on September 2, 1954; later repudiated in the controlled Cairo press. *See* Kirk, "The Turco-Egyptian Flirtation of Autumn 1954," *The World Today,* no. 12 (1956), pp. 449–50.

9. *See* Mark Alexander (pseud. of Walter Z. Laqueur), "Shifting Sands," *Twentieth Century,* May, 1954, pp. 409–10. Laqueur put his finger neatly on one characteristic of the regime: "Depending on who their interlocutors are, the members of the Junta take on different kinds of protective coloring; in part this is a matter of genuine, unconscious mimicry. When receiving Mr. Crossman or Kingsley Martin they fancy themselves internationalist, agrarian reformers, or even left-wing socialists. In talking to representatives of such American publications as *Time* or *Life* they sound for all the world like U.S. Republicans, orthodox defenders of 'free enterprise,' and pillars of the social order. One of the few visitors who refused to be taken in was Aneurin Bevan. . . . Other visitors have displayed far less sales resistance."

Laqueur might have noted that this "protective coloring" was once utilized by the Zionists also. (*See* Sir Charles Webster, "The Art and Practice of Diplomacy," *The Listener,* February 28, 1952, pp. 335–36, referring to Dr. Weizmann during World War I.)

But with the Zionists, it was probably a deliberate, planned technique rather than an unconscious one.

10. *See* Lacouture, *op. cit.,* pp. 244 and 254; and cf. the procedure of Arabi's junta in extracting confessions from their Turco-Circassian opponents in the spring of 1882.

11. The Egyptian press had by this time been *gleichgeschaltet* by the Ministry of National Guidance, and there had been outbursts of violent propaganda against Britain on those frequent occasions when the negotiations for a withdrawal reached a deadlock.

12. *See* his *Egypt* (London: Ernest Benn, 1958; New York: Frederick A. Praeger, 1958); and Kirk, letter to *The Times Literary Supplement,* April 3, 1959, p. 193.

13. *See Address by . . . Nuri as-Sa'id,* broadcast from Baghdad Radio on December 16, 1956 (Iraq Government, Directorate General of Guidance & Broadcasting), pp. 7–10.

14. *See* Kirk, *Middle East, 1945-1950,* p. 306 n. 1. Article 10 of the Pact stated: "The Contracting States undertake to conclude no international agreements which may be contradictory to the provisions of this Treaty nor to act in their international relations in a way which may be contrary to the aims of the Treaty" (J. C. Hurewitz, *Diplomacy in the Near and Middle East* [Princeton, N.J.: D. Van Nostrand Co., 1956], II, 311-14).

15. *See* Kirk, "Turco-Egyptian Flirtation," pp. 452–55.

16. For Nasser's implicit claim that he had a "gentleman's agreement" with the United States and Britain that Egypt should take the lead in constructing a "purely Arab defense alliance free from formal links with outside powers," *see* Keith Wheelock, *Nasser's New Egypt* (New York: Frederick A. Praeger, 1960), pp. 221–22.

17. Sir Anthony Eden, who had his first meeting with Nasser in February, 1955, was impressed by him as "a fine man physically," but commented on his attitude to the pact: "No doubt jealousy plays a part in this and a frustrated desire to lead the Arab world" (Eden, *op. cit.,* p. 221 [Br. ed], p. 245 [U.S. ed.]); cf. R. H. S. Crossman, *Parliamentary Debates,* House of Commons, vol. 539, col. 866, April 4, 1955. A satirical account of the Arab League meeting was given by Salāh Sālim in *al-Gumhuriya*; *see*

translation by F. Bertier, *Politique Etrangère,* no. 22 (1957), pp. 541–50.

18. *Middle East Crisis* (London and Baltimore, Md.: Penguin Books, 1957), pp. 57–58.

19. This was in continued Egyptian defiance of the Security Council resolution of September, 1951, which had ruled that the Egyptian stopping of ships passing through the Canal with cargoes for or from Israel was not in accordance with the 1949 Armistice or the 1888 Suez Canal Convention, and had called on Egypt to desist (Calvocoressi and Isepp, *Survey of International Affairs, 1951,* pp. 277–78). The Carnegie Endowment study *Egypt and the United Nations,* by a group of Egyptian lawyers (New York: Manhattan Publishing Co., 1957) omits all reference to these proceedings.

20. U.N. Document S/3373, in Noble Frankland (ed.), *Documents on International Affairs, 1955* (Royal Institute of International Affairs; London and New York: Oxford University Press, 1958), p. 354; and Eden, *op. cit.,* p. 515 (Br. ed.), p. 575 (U.S. ed.).

21. Richard H. Nolte and William R. Polk, "Toward a Policy for the Middle East," *Foreign Affairs,* no. 36 (1958), p. 655; cf. Wilton Wynn, *Nasser of Egypt: The Search for Dignity* (Cambridge, Mass.: Arlington Books, 1959), pp. 116–17.

22. *The New York Times,* July 8, 1955, p. 8; cf. Dana Adams Schmidt, in *ibid.,* August 31, 1955, p. 1, and Abdel Nasser's speech on the confiscation of the Suez Canal, July 26, 1956: "Do we want arms to lead and guide us as these arms wish or as the sellers wish, or do we want arms to be used to realize our objectives and consolidate our freedom and independence? Of course there is no reason at all for us to buy arms and pay for them with our personality and principles" (Noble Frankland [ed.], *Documents on International Affairs, 1956* [Royal Institute of International Affairs; London and New York: Oxford University Press, 1959], p. 90). See Wheelock, *op. cit.,* pp. 145–49, for a discussion of the resulting "heavy reliance on deficit financing."

23. *See* Walter Z. Laqueur, *The Soviet Union and the Middle East* (New York: Frederick A. Praeger, 1959), part II, "The Great Breakthrough" (pp. 189–348).

24. According to the Ankara correspondent of *The New*

York Times (December 28, 1954), the Turkish determination to obtain a precise defense commitment from Egypt, Iraq, and as many other Arab states as possible was "strongly supported by the United States."

25. On December 12, 1955, the Foreign Secretary commented: "No one said until quite recently that the Pact was provocative. That is quite a new idea" (*Parliamentary Debates,* House of Commons, vol. 547, col. 833). The debate of April 4, 1955, had turned almost entirely upon the Pact's effect on Israel (*ibid.,* vol. 539, cols. 834–903).

26. "A surprise to the State Department as well as to Nasser" (John Robinson Beal, *John Foster Dulles* [New York: Harper & Brothers, 1957], p. 249). "Having played a leading part to inspire the project, the United States Government held back while Britain joined it. . . . Worse still, they tried to take credit for this attitude in capitals like Cairo, which were hostile to the Pact. Thus by a series of hesitant steps they drew nearer the Pact, sending an observer and spending money, but still not joining it. An ounce of membership would have been worth all the havering and saved a ton of trouble later on" (Eden, *op. cit.,* p. 336 [Br. ed.], p. 375 [U.S. ed.]).

27. Marcel Colombe, *"L'Egypte et le nationalisme arabe,"* *Orient,* no. 5 (1958), p. 127. A graduating student of the American University of Beirut, asked to define this "positive neutralism" (as its Egyptian authors called it), answered, "Wanting to get your benefit from both sides."

28. *See* Kirk, *Middle East in the War,* pp. 64–78; and Khadduri, *op. cit.*

29. *See* Régis Agostini, *"Egypte et Inde: deux conceptions du neutralisme," Orient,* no. 6 (1958).

30. Speech at Alexandria, July 26, 1956, in Frankland, *Documents on International Affairs, 1956,* pp. 93–94.

31. *See* Gamil as-Sabban (Secretary-General of the Industrial Council of the Egyptian Federation of Industry), "The Aswan High Dam," *Middle Eastern Affairs,* no. 6 (1955), p. 384; and Joachim Joesten, "Nasser's Daring Dream: The Aswan High Dam," *The World Today,* no. 16 (1960).

32. *The Times,* November 11, 1954, p. 6.

33. *See* Wheelock, *op. cit.,* pp. 183–86.

34. *Department of State Bulletin,* vol. 35 (July 19, 1956), p. 188.

35. Eden, *op. cit.,* p. 420 (Br. ed.), p. 468 (U.S. ed.).

36. Speech at Alexandria, July 26, 1956, *loc. cit.,* pp. 97–102; cf. Beal, *op. cit.,* pp. 255–56.

37. Sam Pope Brewer, in *The New York Times,* June 21, 1956, p. 5; cf. Wheelock, *op. cit.,* pp. 186–94.

38. Abdel Nasser had recently affronted the United States by establishing diplomatic relations with the Chinese Communist Government, apparently as a riposte for the increasingly close U.S. association with the Baghdad Pact.

39. Eden, *op. cit.,* p. 422 (Br. ed.), p. 470 (U.S. ed.).

40. Cf. *ibid.,* p. 421 (Br. ed.), p. 469 (U.S. ed.): "Already at the beginning of the year the Iraqi Government were complaining that the Egyptians had done better out of the West by bullying than they had by cooperating." Dulles' biographer refers to the Philippines and Pakistan in this connection.

41. Beal, *op. cit.,* pp. 258–60. The Alsop brothers had commented at the time: "An alliance of Democrats from the cotton states and right-wing Republicans in the Senate opposed the dam project. . . . The least the State Department can do is to use the still considerable power of the United States . . . to cut the Egyptian President down to size" (*New York Herald Tribune* [European ed.], July 23, 1956; cf. *U.S. News and World Report,* February 8, 1957, pp. 82–85). *See also* Roscoe Drummond and Gaston Coblentz, *Duel at the Brink, John Foster Dulles' Command of American Power* (New York: Doubleday & Company, 1960), p. 171.

Chapter 4

THE GREAT DIVORCE

1. Thus characterized by Prime Minister Harold Macmillan on January 28, 1960.

2. *See* Drummond and Coblentz, *op. cit.,* p. 148: "From the start Dulles disliked associating the United States with Britain in the Middle East."

3. Eden, *op. cit.,* pp. 212–13 and cf. p. 208 (Br. ed.), pp.

235 and 231 (U.S. ed.); cf. Drew Middleton's review in *The Times,* February 29, 1960: "Dulles' experience . . . had been in the postwar years when the Soviet challenge overshadowed all other considerations in the making of American policy. . . . One gets the feeling that Sir Anthony failed to give full weight to the strength of anti-Communist sentiment in the United States and to its effects upon the Administration."

4. On the ambivalence of this term, *see* J. B. Kelly, "Sovereignty and Jurisdiction in Eastern Arabia," *International Affairs,* vol. 34 (1958), pp. 22–23

5. "If the insatiableness of man is denied its proper meat in religious faith, then it takes the form of just wanting more and more things and more and more activity to escape the feeling of purposelessness" (Canon V. A. Demant, *Religion and the Decline of Capitalism* [London: Faber & Faber, 1952], p. 175).

6. Strictly speaking, the Sultanate of Muscat and Oman was an "independent state in treaty relations with Great Britain," and not under British protection like the Arab sheikhdoms of the Persian Gulf; but *see* J. B. Kelly, "The Legal and Historical Basis of the British Position in the Persian Gulf," *Middle Eastern Affairs, Number 1* (St. Antony's Papers, Number 4; London: Chatto & Windus, 1958; New York: Frederick A. Praeger, 1959), p. 139, for the realities of the situation.

7. *See* J. B. Kelly, *Sultanate and Imamate in Oman* (Chatham House Memoranda, London, 1959; mimeographed), pp. 4–8, 10–11.

8. J. B. Kelly, "The Buraimi Oasis Dispute," *International Affairs,* vol. 32 (1956), p. 319; *see also* George Lenczowski, *Oil and State in the Middle East* (Ithaca, N.Y.: Cornell University Press, 1960), pp. 142–45.

9. This volume is apparently still "restricted"; but *see* Bushrod Howard, Jr., "Buraimi, A Study in Diplomacy by Default," *The Reporter,* January 23, 1958, p. 14.

10. Kelly, *Sultanate and Imamate in Oman,* p. 10.

11. The Cairo correspondent of *The Times,* February 1, 1956. For an Arab version of these events, *see British Imperialism in Southern Arabia* (New York: Arab Information Center, 1958), part III.

12. Kelly, "Buraimi Oasis Dispute," p. 324. Lenczowski,

op. cit., pp. 145–46, refers to the good offices of the U.S. Government in effecting the agreement on arbitration, but makes no mention of the Aramco activities in support of the Saudi designs.

13. Howard, *op. cit.,* p. 14.

14. *The Times,* January 23, 1956, quoting Saudi documents captured by the British at Buraimi; cf. *The New York Times,* January 27, 1956, p. 4.

15. Lenczowski, *op. cit.,* p. 149, implies that Ghalib was helped by the Saudis and Egyptians only *after* his defeat in Oman late in 1955; but this is contrary to the evidence. On the obscure circumstances surrounding Ghalib's assumption of the Imamate, *see* Kelly, *Sultanate and Imamate in Oman,* pp. 12–13.

16. *See* a British Foreign Office statement in *The Times,* October 5, 1955; and cf. *British Imperialism in Southern Arabia,* pp. 78, 84–85. Lenczowski is silent on this point.

17. *See* Howard, *op. cit.,* pp. 13–14, for details of Young's activities.

18. *The Sunday Times* (London), October 23, 1955. Philby later claimed to have warned the Saudis, "You will lose Buraimi, simply because you cannot believe that a good case can be won by honest methods alone" (Philby, *Forty Years in the Wilderness* [London: Robert Hale, 1957], p. 3, and cf. pp. 231 and 239). Two years later still, Philby was asserting that allegations of Saudi bribery over Buraimi "are not facts but myths, and they do not interest me, except as such" (*Middle East Journal,* No. 13 [1959], p. 487); but by this time he was reinstalled in Saudi Arabia and the view expressed was now that of his Muslim alter ego, "Hajj Abdullah." A senior Aramco official who, in a review of Lenczowski's *Oil and State,* declares roundly that "it is at the British door that the blame for failure of arbitration must be laid" (James Terry Duce, in *Middle East Journal,* no. 14 [1960], p. 339) does not allude to these circumstantial charges of Saudi bribery.

19. *The Times,* September 17, 1955.

20. *See Newsweek,* October 17, 1955, p. 58; and *The Economist,* 177 (October 9, 1955), 379.

21. *See The Economist,* 176 (September 24, 1955), 1040; and editorial in *The Times,* October 6, 1955.

22. *See British Imperialism in Southern Arabia,* pp. 80–81

and 86. Here it is stated that it was the British allegations of Saudi bribery etc. on which the tribunal was about to rule when Bullard resigned; but previous Saudi statements had conveyed the impression that it was a "decision" on the entire boundary question under arbitration which had thus been forestalled. *See The Times,* January 27, 1956, p. 4, quoting an official of the Saudi Embassy in Washington; and *Middle East Journal,* no. 10 (1956), p. 61.

Philby remarked only that "the admirable brief prepared by the American advisers of the Saudi Government would have had a very fair chance of acceptance on the basis of law and historical precedent" (*The Sunday Times,* October 23, 1955).

23. Howard, *op. cit.,* p. 16.

24. *Parliamentary Debates,* House of Commons, vol. 545, cols. 200–1. The Saudis alleged that eighty-two persons had been killed or wounded (*The New York Times,* November 14, 1955, p. 3); but the charge was not confirmed by the Arab Information Center paper (*British Imperialism in Southern Arabia*) and may be dismissed as bogus.

25. *Parliamentary Debates,* House of Commons, vol. 545, cols. 1460–61.

26. Howard, *op. cit.,* pp. 13 and 16.

27. Eden, *op. cit.,* pp. 334–35 (Br. ed.), p. 373 (U.S. ed.).

28. *The Observer,* February 12, 1956.

29. *See Parliamentary Debates,* House of Commons, vol. 549, cols. 2111–2334, March 7, 1956; and cf. Eden, *op. cit.,* pp. 342–43 (Br. ed.), pp. 382–83 (U.S. ed.). For an American oil executive's observation placing British subsidies to the Government of Jordan on the same level as Saudi payments to newspaper editors in Jordan and other Arab countries, *see The New York Times,* January 27, 1956, p. 4.

30. The U.S. Ambassador to Greece had evidently taken a different view of the Cyprus problem from that of the U.S. Consul-General in Cyprus itself; *see* Eden, *op. cit.,* pp. 406–7 (Br. ed.), pp. 454–55 (U.S. ed.).

31. Thomas J. Hamilton, in *The New York Times,* March 18, 1956.

32. Marguerite Higgins, in the *New York Herald Tribune,* March 29, 1956.

33. Dana Adams Schmidt, in *The New York Times,* April 1, 1956.

34. Eden, *op. cit.,* p. 336 (Br. ed.), p. 375 (U.S. ed.). For the continuous stream of anti-British venom issuing from Radio Cairo, which was not merely attacking the Baghdad Pact in its "Voice of the Arabs" program but also inciting to violence by broadcasts in Swahili and other African languages, *see The Times,* February 28 and 29, 1956.

35. *See* the President's press conference of April 4, 1956; the comments of *The Christian Science Monitor's* London correspondent on April 5; Stewart Alsop, in the *New York Herald Tribune,* April 12; and the Washington correspondent of *The Times,* April 12. Eden is strangely silent on this episode.

36. Italics added.

37. Eden, *op. cit.,* p. 99 (Br. ed.), p. 110 (U.S. ed.).

38. *Ibid.,* p. 440 (Br. ed.), p. 490 (U.S. ed.).

39. Just as a legal case could be made for the confiscation of the Canal, so Hitler had a legal case for the remilitarization of the Rhineland; and there were those who justified Hitler's annexation of the Sudetenland, just as there have been those who uphold Abdel Nasser's claim to be still at war, though in a strictly unilateral sense, with Israel.

40. *See* Sir Charles Webster, *The Foreign Policy of Palmerston* (London: Bell & Sons, 1951), vol. II; and Francois Charles-Roux, *Thiers et Méhémet-Ali* (Paris: Librairie Plon, 1951).

41. *See* Eden, *op. cit.,* p. 436 (Br. ed.), p. 486 (U.S. ed.); and Drummond and Coblentz, *op. cit.,* p. 172.

42. Eden, *op. cit.,* pp. 434 and 437–38 (Br. ed.), pp. 484 and 487–88 (U.S. ed.); italics added.

43. *Parliamentary Debates,* House of Commons, vol. 557, cols. 1612–13.

44. Eden, *op. cit.,* pp. 445–46 (Br. ed.), pp. 496–97 (U.S. ed.). *See* Leon D. Epstein, "Partisan Foreign Policy: Britain in the Suez Crisis," *World Politics,* vol. XII (1960).

45. "In a letter yesterday to all affiliated organizations, Mr. Morgan Phillips, secretary of the party, said, 'Labour believes that 1960 should be a year of great hope for the African people, but the recent events in South Africa have sent a wave of horror and

indignation throughout the world. It is our duty to take the lead in voicing the nation's protest.'

"The letter said Labour could do much more if they were the Government. The first opportunity to get back on to 'victory road' would come in the local elections.

" 'The way to defeat oppression and racialism and to assist the causes of peace and social justice is to make our party the strongest and most influential in the land,' the letter concluded" (*The Times,* March 25, 1960).

46. "Dulles had proposed Geneva as a meeting place in the hope that on neutral ground Nasser would be willing to talk, but the British insisted on London, and thus it was no surprise to Washington that Nasser refused to journey to his enemy's capital" (Beal, *op. cit.,* p. 266). Cf. Eden, *op. cit.,* p. 449 (Br. ed.), p. 501 (U.S. ed.).

47. Eden, *op. cit.,* pp. 454–55 (Br. ed.), pp. 507–8 (U.S. ed.).

48. Drummond and Coblentz, *op. cit.* Cf. David S. McLellan, "Style and Substance in American Foreign Policy," *Yale Review,* vol. XLVIII (1958), pp. 51–52; and Benjamin Nimer, "Dulles, Suez, and Democratic Diplomacy," *Western Political Quarterly,* vol. XII (1959).

49. According to Drummond and Coblentz, Dulles formed an impression "that Eden was secretly almost pleased by Nasser's retaliatory seizure of Suez. Dulles soon gained the belief that Eden actually welcomed Nasser's retaliation as furnishing an opportunity for Britain to strike back by invading Egypt" (*op. cit.,* pp. 170–71). It is hard to find corroboration of this view in Eden's *Memoirs,* his theme being that force was the last resort.

50. Drummond and Coblentz, *op. cit.,* pp. 172–73.

51. Eden, *op. cit.,* pp. 463–64 (Br. ed.), pp. 517–18 (U.S. ed.).

52. Walter Millis, in the *New York Herald Tribune Book Review,* February 28, 1960.

53. Eden, *op. cit.,* pp. 465–67 (Br. ed.), pp. 520–21 (U.S. ed.).

54. Eden, *op. cit.,* pp. 475–76 (Br. ed.), pp. 530–31 (U.S. ed.).

55. This consisted of the payment of Canal transit dues into a suspense account, instead of to the confiscatory Egyptian Government as it demanded.

56. Eden, *op. cit.*, pp. 479–82 (Br. ed.), pp. 534–36 (U.S. ed.).

57. *Department of State Bulletin,* vol. 35 (1956), pp. 479 and 481.

58. Dulles had remarked: "I do not recall . . . just exactly what Sir Anthony Eden said on this point" (*ibid.*, p. 481).

59. Eden, *op. cit.*, pp. 483–84 (Br. ed.), pp. 539–40 (U.S. ed.); italics added.

60. Eden, *op. cit.*, pp. 490–92 (Br. ed.), pp. 547–50 (U.S. ed.).

61. *Ibid.*, p. 498 (Br. ed.), p. 556 (U.S. ed.).

62. *Department of State Bulletin,* vol. 352 (1956), p. 577.

63. For Dulles' insistence in August on excluding Panama from the London conference, notwithstanding that her "flag of convenience" made the Panamanian merchant fleet the sixth largest in the world, *see* John D. Martz, *Central America, The Crisis and the Challenge* (Chapel Hill, N.C.: University of North Carolina Press, 1959), pp. 312–13; and cf. Eden, *op. cit.*, p. 435 (Br. ed.), p. 485 (U.S. ed.).

64. *See* Beal, *op. cit.*, p. 270, for confirmation that the State Department was "somewhat annoyed" with its "allies."

65. Eden, *op. cit.*, pp. 499 and 501–3 (Br. ed.), pp. 577 and 560–62 (U.S. ed.); italics added.

66. Eden, *op. cit.*, pp. 504–6 (Br. ed.), pp. 563–65 (U.S. ed.).

67. The Rt. Hon. Hugh Gaitskell, February 11 and 22, 1960.

68. Martin Wight, "Brutus in Foreign Policy: The Memoirs of Sir Anthony Eden," *International Affairs,* vol. 36 (1960), p. 309.

69. Eden, *op. cit.*, pp. 509–10 (Br. ed.), pp. 568–69 (U.S. ed.).

70. For the beginnings of the *fedayeen* raids, *see* above, chap. 3.

71. For the crescendo of *fedayeen* attacks from Jordan and Israeli counteraction during September-October, *see* I. S. Macadam (ed.), *Annual Register of World Events, 1956* (New

York: Longmans, Green & Co., 1956), pp. 298–99; and cf. below, pp. 108–9.

72. Eden, *op. cit.,* pp. 511–13 (Br. ed.), pp. 570–72 (U.S. ed.); italics added.

73. *See* Merry and Serge Bromberger, *Les Secrets de l'expédition d'Egypte* (Paris: Les quatre fils Aymon, 1957), pp. 46–47 and 54–56; and J.-R. Tournoux, *Secrets d'Etat* (Paris: Librairie Plon, 1960), pp. 156–58; the suggestion is that the British, by choice, "held the dummy hand."

74. Beal, *op. cit.,* p. 276; cf. Drummond and Coblentz, *op. cit.,* pp. 173–74.

75. *See* above, pp. 57 and 66. The British were now getting from the United States the treatment that they themselves had given the Free French in the Levant, 1941–45. "Our turn today, yours tomorrow," as Georges Bidault had then said.

76. Described by Dean Acheson as "the sanctimonious self-righteousness which, joined with a sly worldliness, beclouds the dangers and opportunities of our time with an unctuous film" (*Power and Diplomacy* [Cambridge, Mass.: Harvard University Press, 1958], p. 137).

77. Eden, *op. cit.,* p. 518 (Br. ed.), pp. 578–79 (U.S. ed.).

78. President Eisenhower at his press conference on January 26, 1960.

79. *See* his admission of such a lapse at his press conference on February 3, 1960.

80. Beal, *op. cit.,* pp. 276–77.

81. The Chairman of the Board of Directors of the American Friends of the Middle East, on the other hand, could call for "a policy based squarely on moral considerations and upon the American national interest," as if these were axiomatically identical (*see* Philip W. Thayer, *Tensions in the Middle East* [Baltimore, Md.: The Johns Hopkins Press, 1958], p. 94).

82. Since Abdel Nasser had continuously proclaimed that a state of war existed between Egypt and Israel and had boasted of the *fedayeen* raids across the armistice line, it is difficult to see how the Israeli action constituted "aggression."

83. Eden, *op. cit.,* pp. 524–26 and 529–30 (Br. ed.), pp. 584–85, 586–87, and 592 (U.S. ed.); italics added.

84. Richard P. Stebbins (ed.), *The United States in World*

Affairs (New York: Harper & Brothers, 1956), p. 327. *See* James Eayrs, *Canada in World Affairs: October 1955 to June 1957* (Toronto and New York: Oxford University Press, 1959), pp. 256 ff., for a description of the evolution of Canadian policy and its disagreement with U.S. hastiness.

85. "Anglo-Saxon Attitudes" (a review of Eden's *Memoirs*), *The Times Literary Supplement,* March 4, 1960, p. 138.

86. Eden, *op. cit.,* pp. 540–41 (Br. ed.), pp. 604–6 and 609 (U.S. ed.).

87. Stebbins, *loc. cit.*

88. A British journalist (George Lichtheim, in *Commentary,* vol. 22 [1956], p. 511) remarked: "Possibly the whole furor is evidence that the British are still sound at heart; certainly it disclosed that a good many liberal intellectuals are a little soft in the head. But then that is not exactly a new discovery." It was, indeed, no discovery to Zionists, who had been systematically exploiting that same softness for the past forty years.

89. Eden, *op. cit.,* pp. 546–47 (Br. ed.), p. 611 (U.S. ed.). Cf. Epstein, "Partisan Foreign Policy," pp. 221–22.

90. Eden, *op. cit.,* pp. 553–55 (Br. ed.), pp. 619–21 (U.S. ed.); italics added.

91. "From the start, thoughtful people in this country thought it disgusting. . . . The police action has seriously misfired. . . . By last week it was clear that these operations had been a total failure" (*New Statesman,* vol. 54 [1957], p. 165).

92. Eden, *op. cit.,* pp. 554 and 556–57 (Br. ed.), pp. 620 and 623–24; cf. Drummond and Coblentz, *op. cit.,* p. 175.

93. "Anglo-Saxon Attitudes," *loc. cit.*

94. Eden, *op. cit.,* pp. 558–59 (Br. ed.), p. 625 (U.S. ed.).

95. Eden, *op. cit.,* pp. 561–63 (Br. ed.), pp. 628–31 (U.S. ed.). Cf. Tournoux, *op. cit.,* pp. 173–74. If these accounts are to be trusted, it would seem that "the confusion which prevailed at Downing Street" (Drummond and Coblentz, *op. cit.,* p. 175) was not confined to one side of the Atlantic only. The tone of the President's previous telephone calls to London had been one of "extreme tension and irritation" (Drummond and Coblentz, *op. cit.,* p. 174).

96. The Assistant Secretary of State for Near Eastern, South

Asian, and African Affairs was William M. Rountree, who had been promoted to this office from Deputy Assistant on July 26, 1956. He had served in the Middle East Supply Center during World War II and had been Administrative Officer to the Anglo-American Committee of Inquiry on Palestine, 1945–46; he had also served in Turkey and Iran.

97. Washington correspondents reported the skepticism of State Department officials when the British Government drew attention to the large-scale Soviet arming of Syria.

98. "Russia could put down Hungary, the United States could put down Guatemala, but Great Britain and France could not put down Egypt . . . because [they] were weaker than Russia or America (let alone both together)" (Sir William Hayter [former British Ambassador to Moscow], in *The Observer,* February 28, 1960).

99. For the realistic and staunch attitude of Prime Minister Robert Gordon Menzies, *see* his *Speech Is of Time* (London: Cassell & Co., 1958), part III. Eden mentions a "strange" suggestion that emanated from the British Broadcasting Corporation when Menzies (in London during August, 1956) had made a television commentary on the Suez situation, that "to balance the presentation of views" a counterstatement should be made by the eccentric Emrys Hughes, M.P. (Eden, *op. cit.,* p. 448 [Br. ed.], p. 500 [U.S. ed.]).

100. This was the first manifestation of the cancer from which Mr. Dulles died two and a half years later.

101. Eden, *op. cit.,* pp. 564–67 (Br. ed.), pp. 632–35 (U.S. ed.); italics added. Cf. Tournoux, *op. cit.,* p. 174. For Dulles' alleged contention six weeks later that "failure by the United States to halt the Suez invasion would . . . have led to proliferating military conflicts" in the Far East and Eastern Europe, with "the holocaust of World War III" as the "inevitable result," *see* Drummond and Coblentz, *op. cit.,* pp. 176–77.

102. Eden, *op. cit.,* pp. 571–72 (Br. ed.), pp. 637–40 (U.S. ed.).

103. *See,* for example, Nolte and Polk, *op. cit.*; Richard D. Robinson, "What Is Nasser Like?," *Foreign Policy Bulletin,* vol. 38 (1958); Caractacus (pseud.), *Revolution in Iraq* (London: Victor Gollancz, 1958).

104. Walter Millis, in the *New York Herald Tribune Book Review,* February 28, 1960.

105. Drew Middleton, in *The Times* (London), February 29, 1960.

106. *See* below, chap. 7.

107. Eden, *op. cit.,* p. 578 (Br. ed.), pp. 646–47 (U.S. ed.); Dulles quoted in Drummond and Coblentz, *op. cit.,* p. 193. In his review in *The Observer,* Sir William Hayter challenged the validity of Eden's comparison of the 1958 and 1956 situations, on the grounds that "the Jordanian and Lebanese Governments asked for British and American troops." But this disregards the elementary fact that Abdel Nasser's propaganda machine was daily telling the pan-Arabs that those two governments had forfeited their right to exist. He was still the apostle of violent change in the Middle East. The difference was that the United States, which cooperated in checking him in 1958, had deserted her allies in 1956.

108. Cf. Campbell, *op. cit:* (1958 ed.), p. 120: "The strong stand of the United States against . . . its major European allies, *in the absence of any previously formulated and plainly understood American determination* to keep Soviet power out of the area . . ." (italics added).

109. *Department of State Bulletin,* vol. 36 (February 20, 1957), p. 390.

110. "Parity of national, even personal, decision in set spheres of influence" (editorial in *The Economist,* vol. 194 [March 5, 1960], p. 876).

111. Colonel R. Meinertzhagen, *Middle East Diary, 1917–1956* (London: Cresset Press, 1959), p. 294; diary entry of October 8, 1956.

112. Drew Middleton (London correspondent for *The New York Times*), in *The Times,* February 29, 1960.

113. Eden, *op. cit.,* p. 133 (Br. ed.), p. 150 (U.S. ed.); cf. Drummond and Coblentz, *op. cit.,* p. 148.

114. After the 1960 summit conference fiasco, an editorial in *The Times* remarked: "The Americans . . . can preach self-denial and practice self-interest. They seem to think there are parts of the world to be saved from their allies as fully as from their enemies" (May 19, 1960).

115. The previous occasions were President Roosevelt's

"ganging-up" with Stalin against Churchill at the Tehran Conference (November, 1943) and the U.S.-U.S.S.R. harmony over the creation of Israel in 1947–48.

116. *See* below, pp. 167–71.

Chapter 5

THE SMOTHERING OF SYRIA

1. *See* Albert H. Hourani, *Syria and Lebanon* (Royal Institute of International Affairs; London and New York: Oxford University Press, 1946), pp. 191 and 194.

2. *See* Khadduri, *op. cit.,* p. 126.

3. Reference has been made above (p. 24) to this party under its former name of Hizb al-Qawmi as-Suri (Syrian National Party). It had recently changed its name to al-Hizb al-Qawmi al-Ijtima'i (National Social Party).

4. *See* Simon Jargy, *"Le déclin d'un parti," Orient,* no. 11 (1959), pp. 27–28.

5. *See The New York Times,* August 5, 1956, pp. 1 and 18.

6. According to Michel Aflaq, cited by Jargy, *"Le déclin d'un parti,"* pp. 28–29 and 31.

7. *See* editorial in *The Times,* June 12, 1956, for a discussion of the conservatives' "demoralization" in the face of the social revolution proclaimed by the Egyptian junta and its flirtation with the U.S.S.R. at this time.

8. For a discussion of this incident, *see* Lenczowski, *op. cit.,* pp. 289 and 325.

9. *Oriente Moderno,* vol. 36 (1956), pp. 694–95, quoting *an-Nasr* (Damascus), November 25, 1956.

10. It should be remembered that, ever since the formation of the Baghdad Pact, there had been constant incitement by the Ba'th and its friends in the Egyptian military junta directed to the Iraqi nationalists to overthrow the government of Nuri as-Sa'id; from Nuri's point of view, he was acting in self-defense. Cf. Lord Birdwood, *Nuri as-Sa'id* (London: Cassell & Co., 1959), pp. 246 and 261; Benjamin Shwadran, "The Power Struggle in Iraq," *Middle Eastern Affairs,* vol. 11 (1960), p. 116.

11. *See Oriente Moderno,* vol. 37 (1957), pp. 112–13, based on *an-Nasr* (Damascus).

12. Dana Adams Schmidt (Beirut correspondent), in *The New York Times,* March 24, 1957.

13. *See* below, chap. 6.

14. *Oriente Moderno,* vol. 37 (1957), p. 438, based on *al-Ba'th.*

15. Claire Sterling, "Syria: Communism, Nasserism, and a Man Named Serraj," *The Reporter,* June 27, 1957, p. 16.

16. *Oriente Moderno,* vol. 37 (1957), pp. 437 and 571.

17. *Ibid.,* p. 439, reporting *an-Nasr,* July 1, 1959.

18. Paul Johnson, "The Struggle for the Middle East; Part I: America Takes Over," *New Statesman,* July 6, 1957, p. 21.

19. The informer, a Syrian army captain, stated that he had been told by the Syrian Military Attaché to Italy, while visiting Damascus, that the new Syrian Government would receive $300–400 million from the U.S. and permission to take over Lebanon and settle the questions of Syria and Iraq (*Oriente Moderno,* vol. 37 [1957], pp. 563–64, reporting *an-Nasr*).

20. *The New York Times,* August 22, 1957, pp. 1 and 10; President Eisenhower, when questioned at his press conference, was characteristically vague (*ibid., p.* 14).

21. *Ibid.,* September 8, 1957, p. 3.

22. *Ibid.,* September 9, 1957, p. 3; September 10, 1957, p. 9; September 11, 1957, p. 10; and cf. the Beirut correspondent of *The Times,* August 26 and September 16, 1957.

23. *Oriente Moderno,* vol. 37 (1957), pp. 632–33, quoting *an-Nasr,* September 15, 1957. For a presentation (by a sympathetic British journalist) of the pan-Arab view of these events and a critical examination of his argument, *see* Kirk, "The Syrian Crisis of 1957—Fact and Fiction," *International Affairs,* vol. 36 (1960).

24. Moshe Perlmann, "The Syrian Affair," *Middle Eastern Affairs,* vol. 8 (1957) p. 407.

25. *See* Paolo Minganti, *"Considerazioni sull'unione fra Siria ed Egitto," Oriente Moderno,* vol. 38 (1958), pp. 101–6; and Simon Jargy, *"La Syrie, province de la République arabe unie," Orient,* no. 8 (1958), pp. 23–24.

26. *See* below, chaps. 6 and 7.

27. *See* J. Harris Proctor, "The Legislative Activity of the Egyptian National Assembly of 1957-8," *Parliamentary Affairs,* vol. 13 (1960).

28. *See* Anwar as-Sadat, *"L'Union nationale,"* *Orient,* no. 8 (1958).

29. Jargy, *"Le déclin d'un parti,"* p. 31.

30. *See* below, chap. 8.

31. Jargy, *"Le déclin d'un parti,"* p. 32.

32. *Ibid.,* pp. 32–33; *see* Harry B. Ellis, "U.A.R. Booster Party Somersaults in Syria," *The Christian Science Monitor,* August 10, 1959.

33. Marcel Colombe, *"La mission à Damas du maréchal égyptien Abd al-Hakim Amer,"* *Orient,* no. 12 (1959); *see* p. 32 for the *Gauleiter* allusion.

34. Ellis (from Beirut), in *The Christian Science Monitor,* October 22, 1959.

35. *See* A. J. Meyer, *Middle Eastern Capitalism* (Cambridge, Mass.: Harvard University Press, 1959), pp. 4–5.

36. Ellis, in *The Christian Science Monitor,* October 29, 1959.

37. "Syrian Progress Within Union," *The Times,* May 26, 1960.

38. *The Times,* September 29, 1960; *see* above, pp. 93–95.

Chapter 6

JORDANIA PHOENIX

1. Glubb states that he had been aware that his position, and that of the other British officers, had become a political anachronism, but that as a consequence of the very recent expansion of the Jordanian Army, there were no senior Arab officers with adequate experience to take over without a loss of efficiency that might be disastrous in the event of hostilities with Israel. Plans had been submitted to King Husain for a phased transfer of command to Arab officers over the years 1955-61 (Glubb, *A Soldier with the Arabs* [London: Hodder & Stoughton, 1957; New York: Harper & Brothers, 1958], pp. 386–88).

2. "I replied that it would not be feasible to make him a brigadier. Only eighteen months before, he had been a captain" (*ibid.*, p. 256).

3. *Ibid.*, pp. 293–94 and 431.

4. For the Egyptian resort to forgery to incite sedition among the Jordanian army officers, *see ibid.*, pp. 412–13.

5. This would conflict with Abdel Nasser's thesis (*see* above, p. 189 n. 16) that Egypt should take the lead in constructing a "purely Arab defense alliance free from formal links with outside powers."

6. *Ibid.*, pp. 391–92; cf. Eden, *op. cit.*, pp. 341–47 (Br. ed.), pp. 381–88 (U.S. ed.).

7. *See* Ann Dearden, *Jordan* (London: Robert Hale, 1958), pp. 107–8.

8. *Ibid.*, pp. 123–24. Abu Nuwar's "genuine desire to avoid causing trouble on the frontier was thwarted by the meddlesome Egyptians. . . . Their military attaché in Amman . . . began to train murder squads to carry out *fedayeen* raids across Jordan's frontier" (*ibid.*, pp. 141–42).

9. *See* above, p. 72, quoting Sir Anthony Eden.

10. Dearden, *op. cit.*, pp. 124–25.

11. *See* above, pp. 74–75, quoting Eden.

12. According to information cited by Glubb (*op. cit.*, pp. 434–35), these elements had conspired to force the King's abdication by a military *coup* on April 7 which miscarried; cf. *Oriente Moderno*, vol. 37 (1957), pp. 302–3, citing an interview given by King Husain to *L'Orient* (Beirut).

13. William S. White (Washington correspondent), in *The New York Times*, April 26, 1957, p. 3.

14. April 28, 1957. For the role of the U.S. in this Jordanian counterrevolution, *see* Benjamin Shwadran, *Jordan: A State of Tension* (New York: Council for Middle Eastern Affairs Press, 1959), pp. 355–58.

15. *The New York Times*, April 25, 1957, p. 13.

16. *See United States Foreign Policy, Middle East*, Staff Study prepared for the Committee on Foreign Relations, U.S. Senate, 86th Congress, 2d Session (Washington: U.S. Government Printing Office, June 9, 1960), pp. 14–16.

Chapter 7

THE LEBANESE CIVIL WAR

1. Macadam (ed.), *Annual Register of World Events, 1957* (New York: Longmans, Green & Co., 1957), p. 288.

2. *See* Philip Khuri Hitti, *Lebanon in History* (New York: St. Martin's Press, 1957), chap. xxiv.

3. *See* Sir E. Llewelyn Woodward and Rowan Butler, *Documents on British Foreign Policy, 1919-1939* (London: Her Majesty's Stationery Office), series I, vol. IV (1952) no. 199, p. 288, and no. 300, pp. 439–40.

4. *See* Pierre Rondot, *Les Institutions politiques du Liban* (Paris: Maisonneuve, 1947), pp. 25-27.

5. Likewise, those Druze who in the nineteenth century had emigrated eastward to the Jebel Druze (more correctly, Jabal ud-Duruz) showed no great enthusiasm at being governed by carpet-baggers from Damascus (*see* Hourani, *op. cit.,* p. 214); and in the Palestine War of 1948, the Israelis received military support from the Druze of Western Galilee against the Muslims.

6. K. S., "The Lebanese Crisis in Perspective," *The World Today,* no. 14 (1958), p. 372.

7. *Ibid.,* p. 373.

8. The Electoral Law of 1960 provided for a Chamber of Deputies numbering ninety-nine, to be formed as follows: thirty Maronites, twenty Sunni Muslims, nineteen Shi'i Muslims, eleven Orthodox Christians, six Catholics of the Byzantine rite (so-called "Greek Catholics," though they are all Arabic-speaking, as are the Orthodox), six Druze, four Armenian Gregorians, one Armenian Catholic, one Protestant, and one representing the "minorities" (Roman Catholic, Jewish, etc.). The largest single electoral district, Beirut No. 1, had to return three Armenian Gregorians, one Maronite, one Orthodox, one "Greek Catholic," one Armenian Catholic, and one Protestant. In a previous election, a candidate who declared himself an atheist Communist had been allowed to be nominated only as a candidate for a Sunni seat, since this had been his father's religion.

9. *See* Francis Nour, *"Particularisme libanais et nationalisme*

arabe," Orient, no. 7 (1958), pp. 33–36; and Pierre Rondot, in *Revue Française de Science Politique,* vol. VII (1957) p. 83.

10. The centenary of the adoption of the dogma of her Immaculate Conception.

11. *See The New York Times,* November 21, 1954, p. 19.

12. The traditional clientele dependent on a patron; now politically directed.

13. K. S., "Lebanese Crisis in Perspective," p. 375.

14. *Ibid.,* p. 369 n. 4.

15. *See* "Shall Lebanon Copy Nasser?" (by the special correspondent in Beirut), *The Economist,* vol. 180 (September 29, 1956), pp. 1058–59; *The Times,* October 3, 1956, p. 10; and a letter from Salam himself, in *The Times,* October 10, 1956, p. 11.

16. *See* Sam Pope Brewer (from Beirut), in *The New York Times,* September 1, 1956, p. 3, and September 3, 1956, p. 2; and *The Times,* October 3, 1956, p. 10.

17. Iraq and Jordan, having treaty relations with Britain, broke with France only, and there was a hint at the time that Lebanon might, in turn, break with Britain only.

18. *See* Paolo Minganti, *"In margine alla crisi libanese," Oriente Moderno,* vol. 38 (1958), pp. 492–93, and cf. p. 399 with n. 2; and Jean-Pierre Alem, *"Troubles insurrectionnels au Liban," Orient,* no. 6 (1958), pp. 37–38. For the version of the Sunni dissidents, *see* Walid al-Khalidi (Salam's brother-in-law), in *Middle East Forum,* vol. 34, no. 4 (1959), p. 34.

19. Cf. Kamil Abd ur-Rahim, Permanent Representative of the League of Arab States in the U.S.: "Another more subtle but malignant way of causing a breach in the Arab wall of unity is the so-called 'Anti-Communist Doctrine.' Lebanon was about to be drawn into its web. Its salvation was achieved only by a violent internal civil war [*sic*]. . . . Lebanon was saved through the courage of her own children from being drawn outside the orbit of Arab unity" (*Arab News and Views* [New York: Arab Information Center], vol. VI, no. 5 [March 1, 1960]).

20. For the basis of these grudges, *see* Alem, *op. cit.,* pp. 41–42; Nabih Amin Faris, "Reflections on the Lebanese Crisis," *SAIS Review* (Johns Hopkins University), Autumn, 1958, p. 12; and below, p. 209 n. 30.

21. Article 49 of the Constitution provided that the President was not immediately eligible for re-election after his six-year term; but this had once been waived in favor of Bishara al-Khuri "as an exceptional case" by a two-thirds majority vote of the Chamber, and Chamoun was credited with planning to repeat the device. The size of the government majority in the new Chamber was therefore an important issue.

22. Nevertheless, this "idealist" (*see* below, p. 125) was reported to have bargained with the President over the terms on which he would have been prepared to run on the government ticket; *see* Kirk, "Elections in the Lebanese Republic," *The World Today,* no. 13 (1957), pp. 262 and 263–64; and cf. Nour, *"Particularisme libanais et nationalisme arabe,"* p. 30.

23. K. S., "Lebanese Crisis in Perspective," pp. 376–78.

24. *See Oriente Moderno,* no. 38 (1958), p. 508, quoting the Lebanese Prime Minister on May 27, 1958.

25. *Ibid.,* no. 37 (1957), pp. 168, 561, 639, 733–34, and 814; no. 38 (1958), p. 508; also Brewer, in *The New York Times,* November 16 and December 25, 1957, January 5, 1958.

26. *Oriente Moderno,* no. 37 (1957), pp. 636–37.

27. *Ibid.,* no. 38 (1958), pp. 138–39.

28. *Ibid.,* p. 141, quoting *an-Nasr* (Damascus).

29. *Ibid.,* pp. 220–21.

30. *Ibid.,* pp. 317–19 and 399–401. "The present Maronite Patriarch (who by reason of circumstances special to his community was not elected by its archbishops, as is generally the case, but was exceptionally the nominee of the Holy See) has, besides the religious qualifications which caused him to be chosen, clan relationships which . . . cannot fail to affect his attitude in the local political contest. . . . He is impelled by his personal links with the clan opposed to that of President Chamoun" (Pierre Rondot, *"La crise du Liban,"* L'Afrique et L'Asie, no. 43 [1958], pp. 50 and 52). The Patriarch later admitted that his support of the opposition, by this time in open rebellion, was not shared by some of the Maronite bishops, but declared that they were in the pay of the government (*Oriente Moderno,* vol. 38 [1958], p. 511, quoting L'Orient [Beirut]).

31. *Oriente Moderno,* vol. 38 (1958), pp. 396–99.

32. Alem, *op. cit.,* p. 42; cf. *Oriente Moderno,* vol. 38 (1958), p. 401.

33. K. S., "Lebanese Crisis in Perspective," p. 378. For an opposition version of these events, the reader may consult an account written by a British "angry young man" of letters—Desmond Stewart, *Turmoil in Beirut* (London: Allan Wingate Publishers, 1958). Unfortunately, Mr. Stewart, like his prototype Wilfred Blunt in Egypt seventy-six years earlier, found it expedient to leave the country before the "turmoil" reached its height, so that his firsthand account is incomplete.

34. *See* Alem, *op. cit.,* pp. 43–44; and *Oriente Moderno,* vol. 38 (1958), pp. 403–4.

35. The army was about 40 per cent Muslim. In the bloodless revolution of 1952, General Chehab had carefully avoided taking sides and had left the matter to be settled by the civilian politicians.

36. Charles W. Thayer, *Diplomat* (New York: Harper & Brothers, 1959), p. 8. The date is given here (on p. 1) as "Sunday morning, May 10, 1958"; but Sunday was May 11, and the day of the week is well established by the context.

37. *See* Ralph and Molly Izzard, *Smelling the Breezes, A Journey Through the High Lebanon* (London: Hodder & Stoughton, 1959), pp. 48–49, 74–75, and 85; this journey was made in 1957.

38. Lindesay Parrott, in *The New York Times,* July 4, 1958.

39. *The Times,* July 1, 1958, report from Beirut. For Egyptian jubilation at the anodyne U.N. report, reminiscent of the Runciman mission's whitewashing report on Czechoslovakia twenty years earlier, *see* Osgood Carruthers (Cairo correspondent), in *The New York Times,* July 6, 1958. A U.N. correspondent admitted a year later that "UNOGIL was not able to perform its observation task in parts of Lebanon until well after the damage, from the point of view of the government, had been done" (William R. Frye, in *The Christian Science Monitor,* August 6, 1959).

40. *The New York Times,* July 2, 1958.

41. Thayer, *op. cit.,* pp. 13, 17, and 24–25.

42. *Time* (July 7, 1958, p. 18) asserted that President Chamoun was the "one man" who "from the outset . . . has in-

sisted on turning Lebanon's internal troubles into an international crisis"—just like President Benes of Czechoslovakia in 1938, one might add!

43. *See* above, p. 130.

44. A new type of popular leader was emerging, however, who "controlled the mob and reduced the nominal leadership to the status of virtual prisoners" (Dr. Nabih Faris, "Report on Lebanon," *Middle East Report,* 1959, p. 44). This type was called *shaikh shabab* ("young men's leader"), a term already current during the earlier Lebanese "time of troubles" (1855-60); *see* Malcolm H. Kerr, *Lebanon in the Last Years of Feudalism, 1840-1868* (American University of Beirut, 1959), pp. 40-41 and 47-48.

45. *The Times,* July 1, 1958.

46. *See* below, chap. 8.

47. Not content with their subversive activities in Lebanon, the U.A.R. pan-Arab agitators were similarly engaged against the government of King Husain; *see* Eden, *op. cit.,* pp. 577-78 (Br. ed.), pp. 646-47 (U.S. ed.).

48. Thayer, *op. cit.,* pp. 29-35.

49. *See Oriente Moderno,* vol. 38 (1958), p. 801. The old gentleman had some reason to feel aggrieved, as there had been two serious terrorist attempts on his life in the past two months (*ibid.,* pp. 714 and 800).

50. Thayer, *op. cit.,* p. 37.

51. "No candidate for Parliament has a chance of being elected, or even of being included on a 'list,' if he is not acceptable to voters outside his own religious community. Only compromise personalities are therefore eligible for the Lebanese Parliament. By this very fact such men are not the champions of their own community or even its most characteristic representatives. Men of too strongly marked attitudes cannot in these circumstances present themselves to the electorate. . . . The communities must therefore have, in fact if not in law, representatives in the state other than the members of Parliament" (Pierre Rondot, *"Quelques reflexions sur les structures du Liban," Orient,* no. 6 [1958], pp. 28-29).

52. Emile Bustani, "An Oasis of Democracy," *Middle East Forum,* vol. 36, no. 5 (May, 1960), p. 9.

Chapter 8

IRAQ REVERTS TO TYPE

1. Stephen H. Longrigg, *Four Centuries of Modern Iraq* (Oxford: Clarendon Press, 1925), p. 321.

2. The Kurds were also predominantly Sunni, but their tribal leaders felt little affinity with the Sunni Arabs.

3. After a period of economic prosperity under the Abbasid caliphate (ninth and tenth centuries A.D.), Iraq had been resubjected to the steady infiltration of tribal nomads during the ensuing "time of troubles."

4. Doreen Warriner, *Land Reform and Development in the Middle East* (Royal Institute of International Affairs; London and New York: Oxford University Press, 1957), pp. 116–17.

5. Elie Kedourie's able article *"Réflexions sur l'histoire du royaume d'Irak"* (*Orient*, no. 11 [1959]) is marred by prejudice, the author being an Iraqi Jew in origin; cf. Christopher Sykes's review of Kedourie's earlier book in *Journal of the Royal Central Asian Society*, no. 44 (1957), p. 57: "Surely Mr. Kedourie is ultimately unjust to the beautiful and absurd figure of the rethroned King. . . . Should he not have indicated Faisal's later and not disreputable career as the first sovereign of Iraq?"

6. Quoted in Sir Arnold Wilson, *Mesopotamia, 1917-1920* (London and New York: Oxford University Press, 1931), p. xi n. 1.

7. *See* Longrigg, *Iraq, 1900 to 1950* (Royal Institute of International Affairs; London and New York: Oxford University Press, 1953), pp. 122–23.

8. *Op. cit.,* pp. 137–38; the entire section on "The Origins of Large Landownership" (pp. 135–38) is illuminating, as is the one on "Settlement of Title" (pp. 142–47).

9. *See* Khadduri, *op. cit.,* pp. 49–51 and 55–58.

10. *Loc. cit.*

11. *See* Khadduri, *op. cit.,* chaps. V–IX.

12. Faisal II had succeeded his father, the ineffectual young Ghazi, in 1939 at the age of four.

13. Notably in the riots that forced the abandonment of the revised Anglo-Iraqi (Portsmouth) Treaty of 1948. *See* Kirk, *Mid-*

dle East, 1945-1950, pp. 155–58, for a discussion of the national-
ist-Communist collusion; and cf. Laqueur, *Communism and
Nationalism in Middle East,* p. 193. Despite this clear evidence,
the Mediterranean correspondent of *The Christian Science Monitor* wrote on January 11, 1960, of "the traditionally anti-Communist parties, including the Ba'thists and the Istiqlal."

14. "He was the most imposing of living Arabs, his fiber
toughened by a Turkish background: and even his unfortunate
opponents, pallid in prison cells or sipping their coffees dispiritedly
on spindly suburban chairs—even those poor victims had to admit
that, unspeakable blackguard though he was, Nuri did at least have
character" (James Morris, *The Hashemite Kings* [London: Faber
& Faber, 1959; New York: Pantheon Books, 1959], p. 183).

15. Contrary to the assumption of many Western journalists,
Nuri was not himself of landowning stock, but the son of a small
official in the Ottoman civil service, and he died a relatively poor
man for a prime minister (*see* Birdwood, *op. cit.,* pp. 8–9, 163,
and 187–90).

16. Longrigg and Frank Stoakes, *Iraq* (London: Ernest
Benn, 1958; New York: Frederick A. Praeger, 1958), p. 241; for
his party's collusion with both Istiqlal and the Communists, *see*
Laqueur, *Communism and Nationalism in Middle East,* p. 201;
and cf. Brijen K. Gupta, "The Objective and Goals of the National
Democratic Party of Iraq," *Middle East Journal,* vol. 14 (1960),
pp. 322–24.

17. Birdwood, *op. cit.,* pp. 276–77.

18. The national income was approximately doubled between
1951 and 1956 (Meyer, *op. cit.,* p. 3); but how far down did this
improvement reach?

19. *The Times Literary* Supplement, 1959, p. 449.

20. F[rancis] B[ertier], reviewing M. Montuori's *Le dé-
veloppement économique de l'Irak,* in *Orient,* no. 12 (1959),
p. 245.

21. Longrigg and Stoakes, *op. cit.,* pp. 188–89; cf. A. F., "A
Year of Republican Iraq," *The World Today,* no. 15 (1959), pp.
287–88.

22. *See* Wheelock, *op. cit.,* p. 51; and Lawrence Fellows,
"Israel Names 23 in U.A.R. as Nazis," *The New York Times,*
September 30, 1960.

23. *Al-Ahram* (Cairo), March 12, 1959; translated in *Orient,* no. 9 (1959), p. 148.

24. *See* Simon Jargy, *"Une page d'histoire de la revolution irakienne: le procès Abd as-Salam Aref,"* *Orient,* no. 12 (1959), p. 85: "An Arab Rapprochement," editorial in *The Guardian* (Manchester), October 3, 1960.

25. Caractacus (pseud.), *op. cit.,* pp. 170–71; cf. Erskine B. Childers, *Common Sense About the Arab World* (London: Victor Gollancz, 1960), pp. 185–86; and Little, *op. cit.,* p. 5.

26. For a subsequent charge by Abdel Nasser that if the first stroke had failed, Qasim had been prepared to support Nuri in crushing it, *see* Benjamin Shwadran, "Power Struggle in Iraq," pp. 110–11.

27. *See* A. F., "Year of Republican Iraq," pp. 290–91; and Jargy, *"Une page d'histoire . . . ,"* pp. 84–93.

28. *See* Shwadran, "Power Struggle in Iraq," pp. 52–54; and Richard P. Hunt, in *The New York Times,* September 24, 1958, p. 10.

29. "The Jester of the People's Court" (by a special correspondent), *The Times* (London), January 25, 1960. For an Egyptian newspaper's implausible version of the proceedings at Arif's trial, ostensibly based on a tape recording made clandestinely and smuggled out of Iraq in a box of dates, *see* Shwadran, "Power Struggle in Iraq," p. 56 n. 15. The faking of "evidence" was something which the Egyptian press under the military dictatorship had inherited from the "corrupt" period which had supposedly ended in 1952; *see* above, p. 206 n. 4, and Kirk, *Middle East, 1945-1950,* p. 136 and n. 1. In 1958, the Egyptian press produced a photostat purporting to show Charles Malik, when he was Foreign Minister of Lebanon, in treasonable correspondence with the Israelis.

30. Georges Clin, *"Situation de l'Irak,"* *Orient,* no. 8 (1958), p. 37.

31. Native to Iraq, as distinct from the unitary concept of the Arab "nation."

32. Clin, *"Situation de l'Irak,"* p. 38.

33. "The chief reason for the Egyptian defeat [by the Israelis in Sinai in 1956] was the quality of the Egyptian officers, their lack of ability, lack of aptitude, lack of keenness, their poor morale and

the absence of any aggressive fighting spirit. The officer, especially the regimental officer, is the mainstay on the battlefield and upon him depends either success or failure. The Egyptian officers flopped miserably in all respects, on occasions blatantly deserting their men when under fire. In the few instances where the Egyptian officers stayed with their men the men fought fairly well, and indeed, in some cases fought on without officers. . . .

"The soft-living Egyptian officers hated the desert, despised their men and generally took unkindly to campaigning. . . . Even the young, junior officer, who might reasonably have been expected to be anxious to win his spurs, was just as unsatisfactory" (Edgar O'Ballance, *The Sinai Campaign* [London: Faber & Faber, 1959; New York: Frederick A. Praeger, 1959]), pp. 193–94; cf. Wheelock, *op. cit.*, pp. 58–59.

34. *See* "The New Iraq—I. Nasserists in Eclipse" (by the Middle East correspondent), *The Times,* December 16, 1958; Jargy, *"Une page d'histoire . . . ,"* p. 85; and Shwadran, "Power Struggle in Iraq," p. 53, but cf. p. 52 n. 13.

35. Fa'iz Sayigh, *Middle East Forum,* vol. 35, no. 6 (June, 1959), p. 33; Sayigh is a pan-Arab propagandist in the U.S.

36. For the "failure of the nationalists to organize themselves as an enlightened group," *see* Khadduri, *op. cit.,* pp. 260, 270, 278, and 363; and cf. Morris, *op. cit.,* p. 182: "The politicians of the opposition . . . wilted away helplessly in grubby obscurity. . . ."

Chapter 9

ABDEL NASSER AT DAMASCUS—OR THE NEW SAINT PAUL

1. *Le Monde,* October 10, 1958, p. 7; and *al-Ahram,* November 28, 1958, translated in *Orient,* no. 8 (1958), p. 179; cf. Wheelock, *op. cit.,* p. 72.

2. *al-Ahram,* November 15, 1958, translated in *Oriente Moderno,* vol. 38 (1958), p. 981.

3. *See* Simon Jargy, *"La Syrie, province de la Republique arabe unie,"* *Orient,* no. 8 (1958), pp. 27–28; and cf. *Oriente Moderno,* vol. 38 (1958), pp. 839–40.

4. *Oriente Moderno,* vol. 38 (1958), pp. 769–70, reporting *L'Orient* (Beirut), August 23 and 26, 1958.

5. *Oriente Moderno,* vol. 39 (1959), p. 35, reporting *al-Ahram,* November 28, 1958.

6. Salam was "indebted in more ways than one" to Egypt in 1958, according to an editorial in *The Times,* August 4, 1960. The same newspaper's Beirut correspondent had reported "cynical amusement" on the eve of the Lebanese elections "over the supposed dilemma of a reputed subsidy source of 1958 . . . as the recipients of two years ago sometimes seemed to disburse [these subsidies] within too close a circle" (May 11, 1960).

7. *See* Jargy, *"La Syrie, province de la Republique arabe unie,"* p. 33.

8. Walter H. Waggoner, in *The New York Times,* December 9, 1958.

9. *See* Harry Ellis, *The Christian Science Monitor,* December 15, 1958; and the Middle East correspondent of *The Times,* January 5, 1959.

10. Al-Ittihad al-Qawmi, whose organization was entrusted to Colonel Anwar as-Sadat; *see "L'Union nationale," Orient,* no. 8 (1958), pp. 157–67.

11. *See "Reaction et communisme en Syrie," Orient,* no. 8 (1958), pp. 188–92.

12. *Ibid.,* pp. 192–94.

13. *Middle East Forum,* vol. 34, no. 4 (April, 1959), p. 45.

14. *"La Republique arabe unie face à l'Irak et au communisme," Orient,* no. 9 (1959), pp. 124 and 126.

15. Nasser was making this speech in the presence of Marshal Tito.

16. Cf. the intransigence of a previous Egyptian Government over union with the Sudan—described in Kirk, *Middle East, 1945-50,* pp. 129 and 134; and Calvocoressi and Issep, *Survey of International Affairs, 1951,* pp. 267–68.

17. *Orient,* no. 9 (1959), pp. 134–35 and 136.

18. *Ibid.,* p. 139, quoting *al-Ahram,* February 24, 1959.

19. *See* Eric Rouleau, in *Le Monde,* February 13, 1959, p. 16.

20. Though this sentence, like those for ex-Prime Minister Fadil al-Jamali and others, was not carried out.

21. Ellis, in *The Christian Science Monitor,* February 9, 1959.

22. An organization of the same name had been created in Syria by the Ba'th during its left-wing phase (*see Oriente Moderno,* vol. 36 [1956], p. 485), but had presumably been *gleichgeschaltet* after the establishment of the U.A.R.

23. *Orient,* no. 9 (1959), p. 145, quoting a broadcast from a Mosul radio transmitter furnished to the rebels by the U.A.R. (*see Oriente Moderno,* vol. 39 [1959], pp. 185–86, translated from *al-Bilad* [Baghdad]).

24. This paragraph is based on Michel Montserrat, *"L'affaire de Mossoul," Orient,* no. 9 (1959).

25. *Al-Qāsim* is properly an epithet of Allah, "the distributor" of destinies.

26. *See* Gaston Wiet, *"L'emblème de la République arabe unie," Orient,* no. 9 (1959).

27. *Ibid.,* pp. 148–51.

28. Montserrat, *"L'affaire de Mossoul,"* p. 28.

29. *Ibid.,* pp. 157 and 159.

30. *Ibid.,* p. 129.

31. This "doctrine of Arab nationalism" (which was, of course, a useful cloak for Egyptian expansionist—not to say imperialist—ambitions) had also provided its devotees with a justification for the U.A.R.'s intervention in the "internal civil war" in Lebanon (*see* above, p. 208 n. 19) and incitement to murder King Husain of Jordan as his kinsmen had been murdered in Iraq. The Tunisian Government, attending its first meeting of the Arab League after its admission, had withdrawn in the fall of 1958 in protest against the Egyptians' harboring of President Bourguiba's personal rival Salah ibn Yusuf, who had likewise been calling for "patriots" to murder Bourguiba.

32. *Al-Ahram,* April 18, 1959, translated in *Orient,* no. 10 (1959), pp. 173–87; regarding the British resumption of arms sales to Qasim's government, *see Parliamentary Debates,* House of Commons, vol. 605, cols. 836–39, May 11, 1959. The establishment in July, 1959, of a chair of Shi'i doctrine in the Cairo University of al-Azhar looked like another move in the Egyptian-Iraqi cold war; *see* Pierre Rondot, *"Les Chiites et l'unité de l'Islam d'aujourd'hui," Orient,* no. 12 (1959).

33. The party had, however, a leftist dissident wing which associated itself with the Communists in a National Front manifesto not recognized by the government; *see* Arnold Hottinger, "An Eye-Witness Report on Iraq," *Swiss Review of World Affairs,* vol. IX, no. 6 (1959), p. 13.

34. *See* Hamilton A. R. Gibb and Harold Bowen, *Islamic Society and the West,* vol. I: *Islamic Society in the Eighteenth Century,* Part I (London and New York: Oxford University Press, 1950), p. 268.

35. Hottinger, "Eye-Witness Report on Iraq," p. 14. It should be noted that Kadhimiya was traditionally Shi'i and Adhamiya Sunni.

36. Johann Caspar (pseud.), "Baghdad's Year of Revolution," *Commentary,* no. 28 (1959), pp. 198–99; note the close verbal parallelism with Hottinger, "Eye-Witness Report on Iraq," pp. 15–16. Later in 1959, when the Ba'th Party had tried to shoot Qasim, it was officially debited with the Kirkuk incident also; *see* below, p. 167.

37. *"Rapport du comité central du parti communiste irakien,"* translated from *Ittihad ash-Sha'b,* August 23, 1959, in *Orient,* no. 11 (1959), pp. 191–93.

38. *Ibid.,* pp. 205–6.

39. When the existence of political parties was again authorized in Iraq in January, 1960, two rival Communist factions applied for registration; the one favored by the government was evidently a minority representing a more nationalist strain of Communism than the majority that took its lead from Moscow. *See* J. Hayworth-Dunne, *"Partis politiques et gouvernment dans l'Irak d'aujourd'hui,"* *Orient,* no. 15 (1960), pp. 87–89.

40. *Orient,* no. 11 (1959), pp. 214–20.

41. Qasim replied in April, 1960, with a boast that Iraq's standard of living would surpass any in the world in *seven* years!

42. Ellis, in *The Christian Science Monitor,* November 19, 1959.

43. Joseph C. Harsch, *ibid.,* October 23, 1959.

44. James N. Wallace (from Cairo), in *The Wall Street Journal,* September 29, 1959.

45. "The probability of another attempt at assassination is openly canvassed on all sides in Baghdad" (Michael Adams [from Beirut], in *The Guardian* [Manchester], December 7, 1959). "Privately Iraqi nationalists are talking of General Kassem's forceful removal as their only way out of the present dilemma. . . . the conclusion, almost universally agreed to by competent observers, that General Kassem is acting in a mentally irrational way" (Ellis [from Beirut], in *The Christian Science Monitor,* December 7, 1959). For the place of such tendentious reporting within the context of the U.A.R. propaganda machine, *see* Marcel Colombe, *"L'Irak et ses voisins," Orient,* no. 12 (1959), pp. 15–16.

46. But *see* Ragaei El Mallakh and Carl McGuire, "The Economics of the Suez Canal Under UAR Management," *Middle East Journal,* no. 14 (1960), p. 128 n. 10.

47. *See* Dana Adams Schmidt, in *The New York Times,* December 25, 1959; Thomas J. Hamilton, in *ibid.,* January 3, 1960; and below, p. 169.

48. This proposal did not appear to have been the work of "Cairo's official propagandists," but was "channelled through to Cairo and sanctioned" by the Ministry of National Guidance (*The Times Weekly Review* [London], December 10, 1959).

49. *The Times,* January 11, 1960.

50. Goaded thereto by Iraqi broadcasts chiding Nasser for his inaction over Palestine. The roles had been reversed since Nuri's fall.

51. It was further reported on May 9, 1960, that the Arab League would discuss a motion to boycott Ceylon tea unless Ceylon broke off diplomatic relations with Israel. Later in the summer, the Iranian Government was denounced for having diplomatic relations with Israel.

52. *The New York Times,* April 23, 1960.

53. *The Times,* April 21, 1960.

54. *See* Lenczowski, *op. cit.,* chap. xiv.

55. *See* above, p. 87.

56. Dispatch from Cairo, in *The Times,* May 9, 1960.

57. For an earlier example, *see* Kirk, "Turco-Egyptian Flirtation of Autumn 1954," pp. 449–50.

CONCLUSION

1. Quoted in Terence Kenny, *The Political Thought of John Henry Newman* (London and New York: Longmans, Green & Co., 1957), p. 140.

2. Oded Remba, "The Middle East in 1959—An Economic Survey," *Middle Eastern Affairs,* vol. 11 (1960), p. 74; and Daniel Lerner, in a review in *The Muslim World,* vol. 50 (1960), p. 325.

3. *The Liberal Hour* (Boston: Houghton Mifflin Co., 1960), pp. 22–23.

4. For the convenient label "nearly-have," *see* W. Montgomery Watt, *Muhammad at Mecca* (Oxford: Clarendon Press, 1953), p. 96.

5. From the *Litany* of Archbishop Cranmer (1544).

Appendix

THE EGYPTIAN LAND REFORM

1. *See* Warriner, *op. cit.,* part I.

2. *See* Wynn, *op. cit.,* pp. 72–73.

3. *See* "*Le Paysan egyptien au lendemain du sixième anniversaire de la révolution,*" *Orient,* no. 7 (1958). For the "profound discrepancies" in official statistics of the agrarian reform, *see* Wheelock, *op. cit.,* p. 81. For some recent modifications of agrarian policy and a favorable assessment of the present position, *see* Gabriel Saab, "Egyptian Agrarian Reform," *Middle East Forum,* vol. 36, no. 7 (July-September, 1960).

4. *See* Warriner, *op. cit.,* pp. 50–54.

5. Arnold Hottinger, "Egypt's 'Liberation Province'—Another Planning Failure," *Swiss Review of World Affairs,* vol. VIII, no. 9 (1958), p. 15.

6. *See* Foster Hailey (Cairo correspondent), in *The New York Times,* March 7, 1959, and an enthusiastic letter from a former legal adviser to U.S. embassies in South and Southeast Asia in connection with the economic and technical assistance programs (Matthew J. Kust, *ibid.,* January 31, 1960); United Arab Republic *Yearbook,* 1959, pp. 222–25; and for more conservative views, Dana Adams Schmidt, in *The New York Times,* November

8, 1959, p. 30, and a British correspondent, G. H. Dempster, in a letter to *The Christian Science Monitor,* December 28, 1959.

7. *Arab Review,* vol. II, no. 3 (June, 1960), p. 40.

8. On this "somewhat expensive undertaking," *see* Wheelock, *op. cit.,* pp. 161–62.

9. Gabriel Saab, "Egyptian Agrarian Reform," p. 44.

RECOMMENDED READING

RECOMMENDED READING

General and Economic

LAQUEUR, WALTER Z. *Communism and Nationalism in the Middle East.* London: Routledge & Kegan Paul, 1956; New York: Frederick A. Praeger, 1956.
———— (ed.). *The Middle East in Transition.* New York: Frederick A. Praeger, 1958.
————. *The Soviet Union and the Middle East.* New York: Frederick A. Praeger, 1959.
MEYER, A. J. *Middle Eastern Capitalism.* Cambridge, Mass.: Harvard University Press, 1959.
NUSEIBEH, HAZEM ZAKI. *The Ideas of Arab Nationalism.* Ithaca, N.Y.: Cornell University Press, 1956.
SMITH, WILFRED CANTWELL. *Islam in Modern History.* Princeton, N.J.: Princeton University Press, 1957.
WARRINER, DOREEN. *Land Reform and Development in the Middle East.* Royal Institute of International Affairs; London and New York: Oxford University Press, 1957.

Anglo-American Relations: The Suez Crisis

BEAL, JOHN ROBINSON. *John Foster Dulles.* New York: Harper & Brothers, 1957 and 1959.
BROMBERGER, MERRY and SERGE. *Secrets of Suez.* London: Pan Books, 1957.
CAMPBELL, JOHN C. *Defense of the Middle East.* New York: Harper & Brothers (cloth), Frederick A. Praeger (paper), 1960.

223

DRUMMOND, ROSCOE, and COBLENTZ, GASTON. *Duel at the Brink,
    John Foster Dulles' Command of American Power.* New
    York: Doubleday & Company, 1960.
EDEN, SIR ANTHONY. *Memoirs: Full Circle.* London: Cassell & Co.,
    1960; Boston: Houghton Mifflin Co., 1960.
EPSTEIN, LEON D. "Partisan Foreign Policy: Britain in the Suez
    Crisis," *World Politics,* vol. XII (1960).
MCLELLAN, DAVID S. "Style and Substance in American Foreign
    Policy," *The Yale Review,* vol. XLVIII (1958).
NIMER, BENJAMIN. "Dulles, Suez, and Democratic Diplomacy,"
    Western Political Quarterly (University of Utah), vol. XII
    (1959).
NOLTE, RICHARD H., and POLK, WILLIAM R. "Toward a Policy
    for the Middle East," *Foreign Affairs,* vol. 36 (1958).
TOURNOUX, J.-R. *Secrets d'Etat.* Paris: Librairie Plon, 1960.
WINT, GUY, and CALVOCORESSI, PETER. *Middle East Crisis.* Lon-
    don and Baltimore, Md.: Penguin Books, 1957.

Egypt

AGOSTINI, REGIS. *"Egypte et Inde: deux conceptions du neutral-
    isme,"* Orient, no. 6 (1958).
BERTIER, FRANCIS. *"Les forces sociales à l'oeuvre dans le nation-
    alisme égyptien,"* Orient, no. 5 (1958).
HOTTINGER, ARNOLD. "Egypt's 'Liberation Province'—Another
    Planning Failure," *Swiss Review of World Affairs,* vol.
    VIII, no. 9 (1958).
LACOUTURE, JEAN and SIMONNE. *Egypt in Transition.* London:
    Methuen & Co., 1958; New York: Criterion Books, 1958.
MINGANTI, PAOLO. *L'Egitto Moderno.* Florence, Italy: Sansoni,
    1959.
NAGIB, GENERAL MOHAMMED. *Egypt's Destiny.* London: Victor
    Gollancz, 1955; New York: Doubleday & Company, 1955.
NASSER, GAMAL ABDEL. *The Philosophy of the Revolution.* Buf-
    falo, N.Y.: Economica Books, 1959.
*"Le paysan égyptien au lendemain du sixième anniversaire de la
    révolution,"* Orient, no. 7 (1958).
SADAT, ANWAR. *Revolt on the Nile.* London: Allan Wingate Pub-
    lishers, 1957; New York: The John Day Co., 1957.

WHEELOCK, KEITH. *Nasser's New Egypt.* New York: Frederick A. Praeger, 1960.

WYNN, WILTON. *Nasser of Egypt: The Search for Dignity.* Cambridge, Mass.: Arlington Books, 1959.

Eastern Arabia: Buraimi and Oman

British Imperialism in Southern Arabia. New York: Arab Information Center, 1958.

HOWARD, BUSHROD, JR. "Buraimi, A Study in Diplomacy by Default," *The Reporter,* January 23, 1958.

KELLY, J. B. "The Buraimi Oasis Dispute," *International Affairs,* vol. 32 (1956).

————. "The Legal and Historical Basis of the British Position in the Persian Gulf," *Middle Eastern Affairs, Number One* (St. Antony's Papers, Number 4). London: Butler and Tanner, 1958; New York: Frederick A. Praeger, 1959.

————. "Sovereignty and Jurisdiction in Eastern Arabia," *International Affairs,* vol. 34 (1958).

————. *Sultanate and Imamate in Oman.* London: Chatham House Memoranda, 1959.

LENCZOWSKI, GEORGE. *Oil and State in the Middle East.* Ithaca, N.Y.: Syracuse University Press, 1960.

Syria and the United Arab Republic

COLOMBE, MARCEL. *"La mission à Damas du maréchal égyptien Abd al-Hakim Amer,"* Orient, no. 12 (1959).

DELESTRE, EMILE. *"La République arabe unie face à l'Irak et au communisme,"* Orient, no. 9 (1958).

JARGY, SIMON. *"Le déclin d'un parti,"* Orient, no. 11 (1959).

————. *"La Syrie, province de la République arabe unie,"* Orient, no. 8 (1958).

MINGANTI, PAOLO. *"Considerazioni sull'unione fra Siria ed Egitto,"* Oriente Moderno, vol. 38 (1958).

RONDOT, PIERRE. *"Tendances particularistes et tendances unitaires en Syrie,"* Orient, no. 5 (1958).

ZIADEH, NICOLA A. *Syria and Lebanon.* London: Ernest Benn, 1957; New York: Frederick A. Praeger, 1957.

Jordan

DEARDEN, ANN. *Jordan*. London: Robert Hale, 1958.

GLUBB, SIR JOHN BAGOT. *A Soldier with the Arabs*. London: Hodder & Stoughton, 1957; New York: Harper & Brothers, 1958.

SHWADRAN, BENJAMIN. *Jordan: A State of Tension*. New York: Council for Middle Eastern Affairs Press, 1959.

Lebanon

ALEM, JEAN-PIERRE. *"Troubles Insurrectionnels au Liban,"* *Orient*, no. 6 (1958).

FARIS, NABIH AMIN. "Reflections on the Lebanese Crisis," *SAIS Review* (Johns Hopkins University), Autumn, 1958.

IZZARD, RALPH and MOLLY. *Smelling the Breezes, A Journey Through the High Lebanon*. London: Hodder & Stoughton, 1959.

K. S. "The Lebanese Crisis in Perspective," *The World Today*, no. 14 (1958).

NOUR, FRANCIS. *"Particularisme libanais et nationalisme arabe,"* *Orient*, no. 7 (1958).

RONDOT, PIERRE. *"La crise du Liban,"* *L'Afrique et l'Asie*, no. 43 (1958).

————. *"Quelques réflexions sur les structures du Liban,"* *Orient*, no. 6 (1958).

STEWART, DESMOND. *Turmoil in Beirut*. London: Allan Wingate, 1958.

THAYER, CHARLES W. *Diplomat*. New York: Harper & Brothers, 1959.

Iraq

A. F. "A Year of Republican Iraq," *The World Today*, no. 15 (1959).

BIRDWOOD, LORD. *Nuri as-Sa'id*. London: Cassell & Co., 1959.

CARACTACUS (pseud.). *Revolution in Iraq*. London: Victor Gollancz, 1958.

CASPAR, JOHANN (pseud.). "Baghdad's Year of Revolution," *Commentary,* vol. 28 (1959).

HOTTINGER, ARNOLD. "An Eye-Witness Report on Iraq," *Swiss Review of World Affairs,* vol. IX, no. 6 (1959).

JARGY, SIMON. *"Une page d'histoire de la révolution irakienne: le procès Abd as-Salam Aref,"* Orient, no. 12 (1959).

KHADDURI, MAJID. *Independent Iraq.* Royal Institute of International Affairs; London and New York: Oxford University Press, 1960.

LONGRIGG, STEPHEN, and STOAKES, FRANK. *Iraq.* London: Ernest Benn, 1958; New York: Frederick A. Praeger, 1958.

MONTSERRAT, MICHEL. *"L'affaire de Mossoul,"* Orient, no. 9 (1959).

MORRIS, JAMES. *The Hashemite Kings.* London: Faber & Faber, 1959; New York: Pantheon Books, 1959.

"Rapport du comité central du parti communiste irakien," Orient, no. 11 (1959).

SHWADRAN, BENJAMIN. "The Power Struggle in Iraq," *Middle Eastern Affairs,* no. 11 (1960).

INDEX

INDEX

229